ORIGINS

CHARLES DORIA is a classicist at large. He has published his own poetry in several journals and anthologies, is the author or editor of four books, and a contributing editor of *Alcheringa: Ethnopoetics.*

HARRIS LENOWITZ is currently Assistant Professor at the Middle East Center at the University of Utah, teaching languages and linguistics. He has published both his own poetry and translations in several journals, and is a contributing editor of *Alcheringa.*

JEROME ROTHENBERG is the author or editor of twenty-two volumes of poetry, including *Poland/1931, Shaking the Pumpkin,* and *Technicians of the Sacred.*

ANCHOR BOOKS

ANCHOR PRESS/DOUBLEDAY

GARDEN CITY, NEW YORK

1976

ORIGINS

CREATION TEXTS
FROM THE
ANCIENT MEDITERRANEAN

A Chrestomathy

Co-edited and Translated

with an Introduction and Notes by

LENOWITZ & CHARLES DORIA & HARRIS

With/ And a Pre-Face by Jerome Rothenberg

THE ANCHOR BOOKS EDITION IS THE FIRST PUBLICATION OF
Origins: Creation Texts from the Ancient Mediterranean.
ANCHOR BOOKS EDITION: 1976

Library of Congress Cataloging in Publication Data
Main entry under title:

Origins: Creation texts from the ancient Mediterranean

Bibliography
1. Creation—Collected works. 2. Cosmogony—
Early works to 1800—Collected works. I. Lenowitz,
Harris. II. Doria, Charles. III. Title.
BL226.O74   291.2'2
ISBN 0-385-01922-X
LIBRARY OF CONGRESS CATALOG CARD NUMBER 74-18844

SOME OF THE SELECTIONS IN THIS BOOK HAVE BEEN PREVIOUSLY
PUBLISHED IN THEIR PRESENT OR REVISED FORM IN ISSUES #2,
#4, AND #5 OF *Alcheringa: Ethnopoetics,* COPYRIGHT 1971,
1972, 1973 BY JEROME ROTHENBERG AND DENNIS TEDLOCK;
AND *Alcheringa: Ethnopoetics,* NEW SERIES VOLUME ONE, #1,
COPYRIGHT © 1975 BY THE EDITORS AND BY THE TRUSTEES
OF BOSTON UNIVERSITY; *Io* #6 AND #23, COPYRIGHT 1969
AND 1974 BY RICHARD GROSSINGER; AND *Panjandrum* #4,
COPYRIGHT 1975 BY DAVID GUSS; ACKNOWLEDGEMENT IS ALSO
MADE TO SCRIBNER'S-SIERRA CLUB BOOKS FOR PERMISSION TO
INCLUDE A SELECTION FIRST PUBLISHED IN *Mind in the Wa-
ters,* COPYRIGHT © 1974 PROJECT JONAH; AND TO TREE BOOKS
FOR MATERIAL FROM *The Pirka and the Pearl,* COPYRIGHT ©
1974 BY JEROME ROTHENBERG.

A hardcover edition of *Origins: Creation Texts from the
Ancient Mediterranean* is available from AMS Press.

FOR OUR PARENTS AND CHILDREN
AND TAMAR

This book owes its existence to the support and attention of Jerome Rothenberg and the journal *Alcheringa: Ethnopoetics.* Much of the material in this book first appeared in *Alcheringa,* and the attitudes the journal fosters have helped us form our work. Other individuals and organizations have contributed to the work and aided us. We thank them for their help, without which our *Origins* would never have been born:

The Middle East Center of the University of Utah, its director Dr. Khosrow Mostofi, its faculty and its secretaries, Jennifer Jensen and Lee Snow
The Department of Languages of the University of Utah and its chairman, Dr. Robert Helbling
The Research Committee of the University of Utah
Charles Olson
Richard Caldwell
Albert Cook
David Matlin
Helen Hickerson
James Whitaker
Sigrid Mayer
Robert Callahan and the Turtle Island Foundation
John Clarke and the Institute of Further Studies (SUNY, Buffalo)
Richard Abrams
Charles Sherry
James and Christina Dengate
Michael Doria
David Guss
the ladies of the Sanchez St. Print Shop
Richard Grossinger and *Io* magazine
Madelon Umlauf
our students at the Universities of Utah, Buffalo, and Texas

August 30th, 1974
12th Elul, 5734

CONTENTS

PRE-FACE by Jerome Rothenberg   xiii

INTRODUCTION   xix

THE TEXTS

PART ONE: CREATION THROUGH WORD

From the Shabaka Stone   3
From the *Pyramid Texts*   8
From *GOD|gods*   10
From the *Hidden Sacred Book of Moses called "Eighth"*
    or "Holy"   18
From the *Poimander* of Hermes Trismegistos   28
Priestly Genesis   37
"Wisdom" from *Ecclesiasticus*   41
The Seven Days of Genesis from the *Secrets of Enoch*   42
Two Stories from Ezra the Apocalyptist   53
The *Sefer Yetzira*   57

PART TWO: ELEMENTAL CREATION

I. RISING   79

A Ritual for the Purification of a Temple   81
From the Papyrus Bremner-Rhind   83
From the Egyptian *Book of the Dead*   87
Fragments from Mousaios   91
The Orphic Cosmogony According to Eudemos   93
The Orphic Cosmogony According to Athenagoras   94
From Pherecydes of Syros, *The Seven Nooks*   95

From the *Sacred Stories* of Onomacritos (?)   99
From Apollonius of Rhodes, *The Argonautica*   120
From the *Orphic Argonautica*   122

II. FALLING   123

  From Aristophanes, *The Birds*   124
  Hyginus, Fable 197   125
  Three Midrashim from the *Pirke de Rabbi Eliezer*   126
  From the Fifth Elegy of Maximian   129

III. DIVIDING: Autonomic and Aliyan Texts   133

  A. *Autonomic Texts*

    Damascius, the Egyptian Cosmology   134
    An Incantation Against Toothache   135
    Damascius, the Babylonian Cosmogony   136
    Sanchuniathon, the *Phoenician History*   137
    Alcman 5 fragment 2 ii, column ii   153
    From the *Homeric Allegories* of Heraclitos the Grammarian   155
    Damascius, the Iranian Cosmogony   156
    From the 36th *Discourse* of Dio Chrysostom   157
    Yahvist Genesis   160
    The Phoenician Cosmogony According to Mochos   162
    Theogony from Sidon   163
    Euripides, fragment 57 of the *Hypsipylé*   164
    The Cosmic Outline of Acusilaus   165
    Fragments from Epimenides, the *Birth of the Gods* or *Oracles*   166
    Euripides, fragment 6 of the *Melanippé*   168
    Justin, *Baruch*   169

  B. *Aliyan Texts*

    Enuma eliš   182
    Berosos, from the *Babylonian History*   237
    Abydenos, two fragments from the *Chaldean History*   241
    The Descent of the Gods   243
    The Song of Ulikummi   246

Illuyanka	262
From Hesiod, *Theogony* (Zeus and Typhoon)	265
From Apollodorus, the *Library* (Zeus and Typhon)	268
From Oppian, *Halieutica*	272
The Battle Between Yam and Baal	273
The Battle Between Mot and Baal	276
The Battle Between Anat and the Forces of Mot	278
The Battle Between Anat and Mot	281
The Building of Baal's Palace	283
YHVH's Battle with the Serpent	289
The Phoenician Orphic Theogony According to Hieronymos and Hellanikos	292
Empedocles, from *Nature*	294
Hymn to Phanes with Proem from the *Orphic Argonautica*	310
From Hesiod, *Theogony* (the Vision)	313
From Apollodorus, the *Library* (Genealogical catalog)	318
The Sethian creation story	322
The Naasene cosmology	327
From Ovid, *Metamorphoses*	335
From Ovid, *Fasti*	338
From Vergil, Eclogue #6	341
APPENDIX: Numerical Creation Texts	
(School of) Pythagoras, *The World of Numbers*	344
Cosmology of the Egyptian Astrologers	352
SELECTED BIBLIOGRAPHY	355

PRE-FACE

What is presented here, these cosmogonies retold, is the paramount interest, & the work of the two who present it is an interest almost equal; & all of it is crucial to the development, the unfolding, changing recovery of cultures & civilizations, that is now to enter its latest phase. Nearly two hundred years have elapsed since that possibility began emerging with the code breakers, the scholars out of Romanticism & driven by the same impulse as its poets, who drew meaning from hieroglyph & wedge, brought the old languages to light—& with those others (searchers & seers again) who needed, demanded, the subterranean & heretical texts that dominant religions & power elites had suppressed for centuries. A historical reconstruction to start with, it was at once more than that: a present concern turned backward, to see the past anew & to allow it to enter into the process of our own self-transformation. "We live," Charles Olson wrote nearly two decades ago, "in an age in which inherited literature is being hit from two sides, from contemporary writers who are laying bases of new discourse at the same time that . . . scholars . . . are making available pre-Homeric & pre-Mosaic texts which are themselves eye-openers."

The gathering that follows has over sixty such eye-openers. Many have never been translated directly into English, almost none (save for an item like the Hittite *Ulikummi,* which Olson himself once handled) into the kind of language that Doria & Lenowitz provide for us here. The change—in the language & structure, the idea in short of what a poem is—isn't peripheral but central, symptomatic of a complex of openings in the aftermath of the two-pronged attack alluded to above. In the paradigm that many of us have come to follow as poets, it's the language that causes us to see, that here can make poetry again from the lifeless things these words were in the first stages of their disinterment. So as the discourse comes to life now in what these two are doing, the past begins to speak through them—at least an image of the meaning & range of the past that no other means could give.

It seems so right here, so alive, that one wonders why it took this long in coming: why, for example, no collection before this had gone back to, translated the available materials around a single topic to provide a "unified field" view of the subject. What happened historically can explain the present situation. Before 1800 our main sources of information for the religion & mythology, the poetry in short, of the ancient world, were classical Greek & Hebrew: Homer & the Bible. Each language had its established works, its canon, & each canon was sufficient to define a classical & sacred tradition: a field for truth & imagination which set the boundaries of reality for man & God. And if our present "curriculum"—whatever classical curriculum remains in schools or on the great books lists—may seem not to have changed much, our actual knowledge has grown through those recoveries that have unearthed & deciphered a score of ancient languages or have revealed alternative traditions in languages already known. Through the nineteenth century & up to the present, specialists have been able to regain & reconstruct much of the poetry of the ancient Near East. And this has led in turn to the publication of poems like the *Epic of Gilgamesh,* the Egyptian *Book of the Dead,* the *Ulikummi,* & the *Enuma Elish:* most in translations that have barely gotten under the skin of the originals or have, as a strategy for recovery of the poem, put it into the language of our conventional & orthodox past.

But for all of that poetic conservatism (& the other conservatisms it has often masked), the historical, mythical, & ethnic realities have continued changing. No longer need one think of Western religion & philosophy as split between two essentially separate traditions: Hellenic & Hebraic. Greek & Hebrew poetry can be read in a new light —shed by literatures older & at least as complex, which paralleled, if not actually influenced, them & which pointed to the existence of an even larger Euro-Mediterranean culture complex. In addition, alternative Greek & Hebrew texts, often outside the established traditions, have continued to come to light: the sacred writings of pagans & gnostic heretics that make an even stronger case for a redefined network of cultural continuities.

Clearly all of this has involved more than pure, disinterested research, as the orthodox defenders, the puritan censors, realized from the start, along with those adventuresome scholars & poets who recognized that the history & roots of our civilization needed to be re-examined & revised in light of the new knowledge. From the latter point of view it was obvious, for example, that such accepted literary forms as epic, drama, history, & so on didn't begin with the Greeks & Hebrews. Not only that, but these categories (the boundaries of which were clearly overlapping) were themselves preceded by an earlier one, the "theogony," & viewed in the light of new concerns with language & function, could be supplemented by forms more in line with contemporary practice: definition, naming, mantra, myth & dream, event & ritual, & so on.

Yet the resistance to popularizing this knowledge was initially widespread: based on prejudices so deeply engrained in the culture that they could hardly be acknowledged until fairly recently. Feelings about Aryan superiority, say, kept many from accepting even the possibility that Homer & Hesiod could have come under Semitic influence —much less the fact. The Greeks had to be narrowly Indo-European or their contribution to Western civilization couldn't be taken seriously. To undermine that uniqueness—blurring long-established distinctions between Jew & Greek—was to strike at the supposed strengths & virtues of Aryan Europe & America.

Religious interests had a parallel stake in maintaining the separateness of the Jewish experience from that of the pre-Christian "nations." And in so far as the scholars were "orthodox" & the texts "pagan" & "heretical," their ideological prejudices hindered translations & studies free from doctrinal & dogmatic preconceptions. In this context it was difficult to empathize with the older texts, to see one's work as part of the transmission of religious & poetic forms that one viewed as superseded or inimical to the "authentic" Christian &/or Jewish revelation. So, for example, many of the "matriarchal" features in pre-Classical & pre-Hebraic literature were treated at best as relics or mere data: even more so when they turned up in Christian works, say, whose initial republication was hedged around by cautionary explications. The puritanism of many of the early editors (or their response to the puritanism around them) also prevented the full & open handling of the erotic & sexual elements in the newly discovered materials—as it had also in long-recognized traditional texts.

Even where much sympathy was present—in Kramer's *Mythologies of the Ancient World,* say, or Pritchard's *Ancient Near Eastern Texts Relating to the Old Testament*—the results, the proof of the work in the poetry, were often ineffective. Almost unconsciously the translators held back, played down their own efforts, as if they were involved in an antiquarian discipline without much interest for the general reader. The language of the translations, the verse itself where verse was aimed at, was too hesitant: the translator as unwilling poet unable to make the leap that would recover the ancient vision & assist the search for primary modes of poetic & religious experience. Or when scholars like Victor Bérard pointed out a community of culture & folkways between Europe & the Near East, their work was dismissed or neglected—this in spite of the use to which Pound & Joyce, say, put Bérard's postulate of a Semitic Odysseus.

But it was among the latter—"contemporary writers laying the bases of new discourse"—that the scope & intensity of the materials were first revealed. Poets specifically & commentators with a less specialized, more universal view of the matter (Olson, Duncan, Snyder, Kelly, Schwerner in his reinvented *Tablets,* Graves & Eliade & Campbell) offered visions of ancient Europes, Asias, Africas, whole worlds united by what Olson called the "pleistocene" or Snyder "the Great Subculture (of illuminati) which goes back as far perhaps as the late Paleolithic." Yet mostly they worked off scattered, bowdlerized translations, taken, *faute de mieux,* at face. The poet's mind supplied the missing force, the linkage: not directly in translation but at a third or fourth remove. The results came first as poems, & that sequence of events may in the long run have set the ground for a new order of translation deriving from the *nous poetikos* as source of energy & form.

The present gathering is a new phase in the process. For the first time the energy enters directly in translation, not as a fluke, an isolated instance, but a full compendium from languages like Hebrew, Greek, Latin, Hittite, Akkadian (Babylonian), Ugaritic (Phoenician, Canaanite), & Egyptian. With their time & place the ancient Mediterranean before the triumph of Christianity & Islam, the editors have concentrated on a central, primal idea, *cosmogony,* the narrative of cosmic origins, & have gathered an unprecedented, range of texts around it. These materials aren't taken as philosophy or theology *per se* but as *poesis*: the making or shaping of reality through speech—myth emerging naturally by way of mouth to ear. The narrative here is constantly in the process of defining itself: not the recollection of an ur-text but mind as witness to its own creations.

To bring across this sense of myth as process & conflict, Lenowitz & Doria, working as both poets & scholars, make use of all those "advances in translation technique, notation, & sympathy" developed over the last few decades, from the methods of projective verse to those of etymological translation or of that attention to the recovery of the oral dimension of the poem that the present writer & others have, wisely or not, spoken of elsewhere as "total translation." The picture that emerges is one of richness, fecundity at every turning, from the first image of poem on page to the constantly new insights into the possibilities of "origin." To the latter end the editors offer a wealth of texts never before translated into English (or translated only in relatively inaccessible scholarly publications), along with more familiar texts reinterpreted:* Lenowitz's polyvalent Genesis, for example, or Doria's reconstitution of Empedocles as "magician, weatherman, & raiser of the dead." Hesiod & Homer, Ovid & Vergil, the Yahvist & the psalmists are here seen freshly, surprisingly, as part of a world with rhapsodic, light-struck Orphists, with Pythagoreans mapping out their worlds through numbers, with early Kabbalists exploring alphabetic powers. The work moves from the simplicity of Euripides' ". . . not my story/but one my mother tells" to surreal assemblages of hidden forms & names: the hermaphroditic Elohim & snake/cunt woman of Justin's *Baruch* (leading by stages to the primal god, Priapus) or that recurrent female body-of-the-world qua dragon whom even Yahveh knew. And this allows that "clash of symbols" which, those like Ricoeur tell us, both is natural to mind & forms its one sure hedge against idolatry.

The editors comment little, but go about the more fundamental process of constructing a world of possibilities: not a single sacred

* All work in the anthology has been newly translated by the editors, with Doria concentrating on the Greek & Latin originals, as well as most of the Egyptian, and Lenowitz on those from Semitic languages, Hittite, and the rest of the Egyptian sources. Among the texts that have never before appeared in English are those from Berosos, Abydenos, Pherecydes, etc. In addition the *Enuma Elish* appears for the first time in a full translation as verse, & several works, like Empedocles' *Nature* or those from the Orphists, represent reconstructions from fragmentary sources. Three translations by myself (Apollodorus [Zeus & Typhon], Oppian, & Rabbi Eliezer) represent the only work by a third party.

work of genesis but a space in which all works can come to light. Here the "imaginations of men's thoughts" are no longer the evil that God saw continually but the reoccurring, strangely shifting *gnosis,* reflective of a wider community than heretofore known, with its roots into that older universal shamanism the West would later try to live without. To get this in the open, Doria & Lenowitz let the words (both of their sources & their own) enter again into that process of becoming—as if to begin anew the old work of *formation.*

And that is so much the achievement of this true source book: its great unifying image for poet & general reader alike. It is a presence still, a power & possibility that outlives the terror of its source. In that way the work is never merely literary, never ancient history, but contemporary with all our other works: the very thing we seek in our pursuit of those particulars, even contraries, that open on the universal vision.

Jerome Rothenberg
Center for 20th Century Studies
Milwaukee, Wisconsin
December 1974

INTRODUCTION

We define myth as any widely held account of how something came to be the way it is. This means that in considering any one particular myth of cosmogony we are actually looking at two main aspects: present condition and past event. In this anthology we've collected and translated the most representative creation stories from the ancient Mediterranean area. Instead of reading them as investigations into superseded explanations, let us rather look on them as alternate realities which may or may not correspond to our present sense of ourselves and our experience—to our own myths. They correspond to old or new sciences.

Myth has this value: it unites rather than separates or divides; it provides ways other than the purely sequential to grapple with undifferentiated experience; it preserves instead of eliminating unfathomed reaches and the discoverable/decipherable spaces that make up at least in part the totalities of our existence (i.e., there are mysteries after all; it is not "all there").

Myth involves public ceremonial of some kind. The tribe, the community, celebrates creation in story and rite because if it did not, creation would stop. Everything would fall apart, collapsing upon itself, returning into unspecialized mass: the primes—chaos or egg. The importance of the public act of witnessing and honoring creation is that it lays bare and reconfirms the patterns of the world. This is the true first cause of genesis (if one can speak of the effect as cause in a world where time sails in a circle, where it is difficult to tell beginning from end). The will to exist is the evidence of creation and sets creation in motion.

In the translations that follow we tried not to diffuse what should not only be apprehended as a luminous whole, but participated in.

For the ancients the world lived, it had present reality. The dead returned their life to the living. In turn the dead called the living back to the grave, so that the dead might once again pass out through the gates of life and death. The soul of the earth had to be maintained and fostered by those who inhabited in what the ancients called "regular sequence" (order=cosmos). If it were not, it would revert and become chaotic: viz. our present "present."

Without regular sequence, fish being in the sea, trees in the hills, seasons circling, mind and eye—all these relations that are necessary for other things—would be impossible for these people and poets. Vital interdependence among the myriad creatures would vanish. The cosmos was not seen simple, a sum of all that exists; it was for these scientists as it is for us, the operations and orders that uphold and sway existence. There are, in these operations, two faces or phases. We are in one phase now (the created), but we could easily return into the other (the uncreated) if we do not make adequate provision through our science, our myth, and its transmission.

The will here is human. There is nothing in the nature of things that wants us to make this apprehension. People make connections and predictions and are empowered to keep things going.

In casting about for a suitable explanation for myth-making, particularly for tales of genesis, we constructed the following schema, reading backward, beginning with Memory concerned in such questions as: "How far away is everything?" "Does distance in time equal past or future?" "Where did it go? and will it come back?" If Memory fails in its task of re-connecting, it too will pause and cease. So, to begin, we say the forgotten explanation (that lost chord) is the earliest myth, the first creation, the accounting of the world as experience.

A new fact, a verifiable and repeatable item of knowledge, enters the continuum of Memory; it reshapes the structure, the assembling of experience in ways re-told through Memory. So the first accounting, instantly renewed through story-telling, repeatedly stirs in us an instinct for knowing. It provides the stories Memory uses to make the transition from this present to the real present; from mechanical moment to living time; from first creation to its recurrence in everyone's sense of himself as in—but not of—any time.

In this way our experience of the world, as Olson put it, becomes the "equal of the real." This includes the stories of genesis; how the world got to be the way it is told to us by the created world itself. When the gods create by word, the worlds they summon into being name *them,* not their creations; so there is no one Standard Version for reality and its Masters.

This must be seen by staying clear inside, by annihilating absolute prejudice and dogma. These are the presents of the recent, not the inheritance of real and returning time. By gaining distance on the beliefs of any—this—present, we can bear ourselves as factually assumptive of our own observation.

The stylist of creation story is this vantage, this look-out through time. It shapes the tales of genesis and gives them point. Here we are seeking a cognate for this, a means of reporting experience to the mythic. Effectively cut off from re-telling the world, we are locked into a cell of our own making. We can only stare out through barred windows at a desirable but spurned world, forgetting that it is made out of the same stuff we are (Adam/red-dirt/Terra). But the need to know is present—to be present at one's own making.

We find it necessary to re-state the value of myth in our literalistic culture. For if people haven't changed all that much since 3000 B.C., their world-views have, leaving earlier myths behind as forgotten residue. "Myth" when it is invoked today most often means "falsehood, naïvism" when it introduces an area of previous cultural contract and belief. All myths have as their subject the origin of something: an object, a relationship, an emotion. Even though later generations may (and do) form their own agreements as to how the world began, these agreements lead directly to the necessary formation of some particular "best of all possible cultures," thus obliterating the "truth" of a previous generation's myth. So the particular objective to which people fashion myths will rarely meet successfully the expectations and needs of cultures outside their own, nor will the myth. A myth will always only be understood as true as it reveals the "truth" about those who tell it.

In the case of myths about the beginning of the world (or any collection of myths) we need a canon. If a researcher wants, he can group Hopi myths as distinct from Zuni; he may separate Sumerian stories from Akkadian, or split Roman mythology from Greek. He groups them in convenient ways: by geography, history, or language. The advantages of such groupings are in the first case, to deal with linguistic developments and interchanges; and in the second, to explore the genetic developments of myth from one society to another which neighbors it in time or place. Both sorts of groupings have readily apparent values, corresponding to the diachronic, but there is another, primary way to group them: synchronically, as a corpus of one type (in conjunction with the diachronic classifications listed above). This typology may serve our purposes better because it interferes least with myth-telling itself, and because it allows us more scope for the presentation of the nature of the cultural/personal compact which allows one myth into our schema at a certain point and not another.

The kind of grouping we are talking about relies on a notion Lévi-Strauss re-formulates: "[A myth's] substance does not lie in its style, its original music, or its syntax, but in the story which it tells." This means that myths (as long as they retain quickening power) develop and change what is changeable in them to fit the needs of that time; while what constitutes the variable is whatever a person holding one variant apprehends in another variant as *the same* myth or story.

Lévi-Strauss oversimplifies the case, for "style," "syntax," and "original music" are all integral to the story of the myth, or are each "stories." We think what can best be learned from typological grouping (plus subordination into language, geography, and nationality) is an understanding of ourselves in relation to the original myth-makers and -tellers. How, that is, they felt such arrangements (now viewing the elements in their stories as incidents) became valid through interaction with themselves while rendering an account of the worlds they presently inhabited and to which they gave intelligible life. What we discover from the typology we use are new points of entry into how people think about themselves both in the present (their "now") and the beginnings (their "then").

The movement that characterizes every creation story is toward ever greater elaboration. Beginning with a massive substance within which no single item is distinguishable from any other, lesser units, becoming progressively smaller and smaller, are made distinct. From the ways in which units become discrete other units can be predicted; binding forces on the same level of distinction can be predicted and isolated. As each schema develops it feeds into the complementary schema.

Through this process we gain some understanding of how people conceive the universe: by begetting it first in their own persons, and then trying it out against the world, allowing their worlds and word to set up a process of dialectic we now call "mythopoeia," a dialectic which continues today. In these terms, people describe and participate in their own development of seeing/doing/thinking by active analogy with the universe.

This may be how man's conception of the universe (intellect) develops itself; man describes the development of perception and manipulation. This side-by-side development of the two schemata is certainly the most convincing explanation yet given to the development of intelligence in the individual (see Piaget's *The Construction of Reality in the Child*); man's perception of the creation of the world (myth) is conceived of as man's perception of the development of his own intelligence. Our grouping sheds new light on why creation myths are alike and the ways they define themselves. There is a possibility that this process of side-by-side elaboration of the manipulable universe corresponds to the growth of the infant mind.

The main groupings for this anthology are *creation through word* and *elemental creation*. These seemed the ones our material suggested, not our willful imposition. We observed secondary categories of nationality, language, history, and so forth inside the two main groupings in hopes of making the typology as informative as possible. These categories seem to hold up about as well as any, and, more importantly, do least damage to the stories and even tell us something about creation story itself, over and beyond narrative summaries of individual tales.

By *creation through word* we mean that situation where the god(s) makes any sound—a cough, chuckle, hiss, whatever they emit as separate from themselves—their first emanation. This sound seeks a response; finding it, worlds come into being and take shape, forming basically the name of the god(s). We chose to begin with this grouping not only because it is the one that all poets and storytellers mime in their essential activity, but because through word the first intelligible separation occurs between the maker and the made; cases in which the word serves as the demiurge, the spirit in service of the god's intelligence. It is interesting that Wisdom, appointed the job of creation in one Jewish tradition, says she issued from the mouth of El the Most High before proceeding to her assigned task.

Our second grouping we called *elemental creation* because we noticed how the very things of these worlds (they are usually fire, air, earth, and water) tend to make themselves in various ways and directions, sometimes with, sometimes without the help of gods. The elements themselves in these old stories are animate and divine, the powers of the sensate world. They survive, among other places, in the djinns of Islam. Only a later, more skeptical age stripped them of their numinous presence, converting them into the elements of the scientist's table.

We further broke down this schema into three subgroups: *rising, falling,* and *dividing.* In these categories we notice how the elements associate themselves in various orders—moving up toward their authors/sources or away from them, or continually dividing and therefore multiplying until the Primary of creation had successfully lost itself in the many secondaries of experience.

We decided that *dividing* took place for the most part in two ways: *autonomic* and *aliyan.* By *autonomic* (from the Greek *autos* meaning "self" and *nomos,* "law or custom") we mean that the world laws itself to go on splitting and dividing because that is its chosen condition. And people have recorded that fact about the diacosm in their mythologies. In the *aliyan* group (from a Semitic root *'al* which means "overcoming") we assemble all those creation stories where the world comes into being because of some fundamental split in divinity which goes on repeating itself through history. This split may assume many natures, but almost all revolve around a generational conflict wherein a powerful but decadent first generation attempts to reassert its dominion and its world, sleepy and dark, over a second generation. In such stories the world, as well as present divinity, is renewed and made young by struggle—as for example in the *Sacred Stories* when tyrant Zeus swallows his great-grandfather Phanes only to discover that he becomes a bisexual being, coterminous with the whole world, uniting in his person the scattered contradictions of time. *Aliyan* itself is a standard epithet for Canaanite Baal, El's son and deputy, who creates the world by gaining power over it from outside, a resplendent hero like Marduk-Assur, who slays and dismembers with his light and air the Sea Mother Tiamat, to make earth, air, and sky. The largest number of creation stories fell into this group, which tells us how closely people felt acts of destruction were allied to those of construction. It is the same dipolarity that turns up in Achilles' ash spear that now wounds, now heals.

We placed in the appendix two representative samples of creation through number. These two tales are not really about creation so much as they are expressions of certain underlying relationships between the magic language of numbers and the proportions they evoke in the world. Yet since they re-produce an important method of fashioning the world we felt their inclusion was justified.

In the titles we include as briefly as possible information about the language and site of the myths.

Part One

Creation Through Word

FROM THE SHABAKA STONE

The Shabaka Stone contains a creation story dating back to at least 2700 B.C. Because of its connections with Memphis, "the granary of Egypt," it is sometimes called "The Memphite Theology." Text: K. Sethe, ed. *Dramatische Texte zu Altägyptischen Mysterienspielen,* Vol. 1. "[. . .]" denotes words supplied.

the gods   in KHEPERA   of Ptah tree column king
               beetle life maker

Ptah THRONE . . .
      [Isis?]

Ptah NUN   father of ATUM
      water sky   sun disc

Ptah NAUMET   mother of Atum
      counter sky

Ptah Great . . . HORUS and THOTH
               Heart   Tongue
                    of the nine [god company]

[Ptah. . . . . . .], - [SETH? . . . . . .] who grew the gods
                    [croc pig]
                              from under his apron

[Ptah. . . . . . .], - [SHU? . . . . . .] who grew the gods
                    [father airs]
                              from under his apron

[Ptah. . . . . . .], - [OSIRIS? . . . . .] who grew the gods
                    [mummy grain]
                              from under his apron

[Ptah. . . . . . .] - [. . . . . . NEPH]THYS lotus
                    nurse cup
                 flowering on RA's nose
                        sun

Tongue
        in khepera   make body for Atum
Heart

strong   the mouth heart guts right handarm of Ptah!

he grew [the nine god company]
shared himself with [them]
            with their KAS   arms upraised
                  food person double
      Heart   where Horus budded
through   . . . .   of Ptah
      Tongue   where Thoth budded
Heart and Tongue won out over [every other] flesh part
                  ruling the [whole] body
teaching [Ptah] is the [Heart] in the womb body
        the Tongue in the bowl mouth
        of every god man beast worm or thing alive
      every one

        there [Heart] thinks
           [Tongue] commands
        whatever he wants

the nine god company [of Ptah] stand before him
        grown into bodies of teeth and lips

[teeth are] the water seed
                of Atum
[lips   ] the lithe spoke arms

lifted from the mouth [of Ptah]
sneezing out SHU   and TEFNUT
      dad airs   ma waters

[his] company of nine grew seeing for eyes
           hearing for ears
           breathing for nose

        giving Heart notice

        Heart who lets all thinking rise
        Tongue to say again all [Ptah's] Heart's thought

that's how every god was grown
Atum and his company of nine
yes every god word
          Heart thinks
          Tongue speaks commands
comes true
the kas lived
the hemsets given places
     ka girls
               bringers of food
               hugging into life
through the words
[Heart thought
Tongue spoke]

[justice rewards] them who act for love
[injustice awarded] those whose acts gain hate
life for the peaceful
an ax in the head meaning death
for those who break the peace

this is the way
all work and art
were spoken into life
right handarms gripping weapons
stepping legs
whole bodies wielding limbs
following the command
Heart thought
Tongue spoke
giving everything
meaning that's why
people say
"Ptah seeded Atum in khepera
Ptah made the [other] gods"

he's named Ptah TA-TENEN
                    god sneeze grower
flailing them
seated

he talked everything out of [NUN]   into food and feeding
                          [first sea]
feeding the gods and every [other] go[o?]d thing
growing himself stronger
than all of them

peaceful Ptah rested
after he'd done

                          every godword making them true
after he'd spoken

under his fox skin apron
he gave the gods birth
his right eye saw the cities into beetle
his pick dug the canals that water the land
he settled the gods in divine booths
drew up what the rent-food men bring them earns
he hoed their chapels' basements
grew them bellybodies
the likes of which
gave their hearts joy

so the gods entered them into bodies
of [every] wood   metalstone   clay   [other kind of] thing
waxing in lotus from [Ptah godearth dweller]
whose forms they pierced

all the gods
        grew together around [Ptah] peaceful delta sand [?]

all the KAS   Upper Land
                          god lord of the
                                          Lower Land

the GREAT THRONE   barns his grain rejoicing the gods' Heart
    Memphis

    the gods in the [reed?] mansion of PTAH
                              Lady of all [   ] life
                              who gives [the wheat]
                              bolstering both Lands

when his water drank OSIRIS
                    grain eye
wife ISIS
    throne
                    watched
sister NEPHTHYS
    cup house

they saw
grief carved them

            Isis
HORUS told   :
hawk   Nephthys
            "don't wait   grab
            get my father out of his water"

the women moved their heads in time
they let him land

Osiris went through the hidden door five cobras guard
into the lion coiled luxury of the eternal lords
where the sun cock shines
                    rays perpetually corded
growing walking
along Ra's high road
falcon head god sitting
wearing the snake wrapped sun
at GREAT THRONE
    Memphis
            enrolled at the gala court
Osiris
        ranked among the gods
            of Ptah TA-TENEN   lord of years
                god grower

FROM THE *PYRAMID TEXTS*

This particular creation story from Passage 600 of the *Pyramid Texts* was found cut in stone inside the pyramids of Mer-ne-Re and Pepi II (Sixth Dynasty—c. 2400 B.C.). Text: Sethe, *Die Altägyptischen Pyramidentexte.*

say in serpent body

:

"ATUM   KHEPERA
  sun disc   beetle life maker

              you climbed the top of pyramid hill
making the light the *bennu* bird phoenix recurring sun gives
in god bird house ON   over universe water bowl
           SunTown
where you shoved out Shu
        spat out Tefnut

                spittle from your lips
                asp rippling waves of the mouth

          putting arms around them
                 clasped them
           in your KA
              double person food

             having them share
            the ageless soul disposed in you

. . .

ha!   strong nine god company in On—

                 SHU
                 daddy airs

                 TEFNUT
                 ma waters

                 GEB
                 lord earth

NUT
lady sky

OSIRIS
mummy fucker

ISIS
cunt river

SETH
sage pig

NEPHTHYS
nurse cup

ha!   Atum Khepera spit named 'Nine Bows' in On
you who never back away from him
offer your heart's shelter . . .

and Atum—protect
protect from all gods from all dead . . ."

From *GOD|gods,* a Greek text written in Egypt probably by a heterodox Jew sometime before the third century A.D. It forms part of a long *lysis* (a ritual of purificatory "loosing" that took about fifty days to complete) from an older native magical tradition. Text: Papyrus XIII in *Papyri Graecae Magicae* (Preisendanz, ed.), Vol. II.

. . .

say :

" YOU

Who sees one and all
Who no one sees

I'm calling YOU
biggestbest GOD
All Maker
Your Own Father-Mother-Child

giving Sun the glory of his blaze and every strength
ordaining Moon wax and wane to keep her paths straight
taking nothing from the darkness born before they were
YOU dealt all equal shares

when YOU appeared splendid in light
the universe was authored
from that brightness
coming into view

all in all subjects itself in order
to   under YOU :

Metamorph : Capable-Of-Every-Form
Whose true body

the gods have never seen

I want YOU : Invisible Time outlasting time
right here

Kyrie/Lord
in good body for me to see

since I slave beneath Your world for Your Angel :
[name] *Bi-ath-yap-bar*

ber-bir   *schhih-lah-tour*   *bou-fhroum-trohm*

for Your Fear :
[names] *Dha-nouf*   *Hhrah-tor*   *Bel-bali*   *Bal-bith,*
Yah-woh

YOU
Who made heaven and earth
stand up together

YOU I want
Kyrie/Lord
right here

since it's from GOD
gods take sight
to start their doing
using *Ech-he-bu-crohm*/Strength-of-Sun
whose shining-prayer-in-praise-of is :

a   *a*   *a*
e   *e*   *e*
o   *o*   *o*
i   *i*   *i*
a   *a*   *a*
o   *o*   *o*

Sha-ba-oth
Zha-gou-reh
Ar-bath-Yah-Woh
god *Arathu*
Adoni

I'm telling YOU
right here
Kyrie/Lord
I want YOU

named in bird :
arai

in hieroglyph :
laïlam

Hebrew :
anochh / I am

Bi-ath-yar-bath   *ber-bir*   *ech-hi-lah-tour*
bhou-froum-trohm

Egyptian :
Aldabahim

like the dog-faced baboon :
Abrasax

the sparrow hawk :

---

khi   *khi*   *khi*   *khi*   *khi*   *khi*   *khi*   *tif*   *tif*   *tif*

---

in priest :
me-ne-foh-if-oth

---

ha   *ha*   *ha*   *ha*   *ha*   *ha*   *ha*

---

now [child] :
CLAP   *CLAP*   *CLAP*

go :
TSWEEEEEEEEEEEEEETSEETSEETSEEE

SSISSISSISSISSISSISSISSISSISSISSISSISSISSISSISSISSISSISSISSISSISSISSISSI

                    come to me
                   Perfect Lord
                 Who knows no pain
                Who pollutes no place
                       why?
                     because
                      GOD
              I have been Completed by
                     and so
                     I Know
                      Your
                      Name
                  ─────
                              ”

[A week of preparation follows. This includes building an altar
outdoors with a tabernacle tent. On the eighth day:]

in the dead of night during the 5th hour
when everything is still
go to the altar of sacrifice

light the candles

put beside it two chickens and two oil lamps ¼ full
(you won't need more than that)

recite the prayer and the GOD-mystery
which is called "scarab the shit beetle"

set out a mixing bowl filled with black cow's milk
and wine without sea water

for this is beginning and end/
drink-offering and sacrifice-eating

write the prayer on both sides of a tablet of natron [*nether?*]

lick one side clean

soak the other in water and wash it in the mixing bowl

use ink of perfume and flowers

before drinking the milk and wine
perform out loud the prayer that follows

then lie down on a mat and listen

pen and tablet in hand do :

" *The Prayer-Hermes-Does*

I'm calling YOU
whole world in Your hands
!!!   OVER HERE   !!!
speaking in all voices and tongues
just as they sang in glory for YOU
that first time
when the world began
for words are Your doing
we believe they are
absolutely true
because YOU are

:

Helios
Sun
[name]   *Ahhebucrom*
meaning——'flame leaps from
Your Disk
like wheelspokes'

I give YOU praise
opening :

a   *a*   *a*

e   *e*   *e*

o   *o*   *o*

YOU made air burst into full
from sunblaze
the stars' white bodies
stand up night
when YOU built and peopled
of light of god
the ordered world

i   *i*   *i*

a   *a*   *a*

o   *o*   *o*

                when YOU
[names] :   *Shabaoth*
            Arbath-Yah-Woh
              Zagoureh
          made the world
          distinct and clear

              Your angels
          who came first to light
              are named
                Arath
                Adoni
              Ba-shemm
              Yah-Woh

Arath cries out in bird
                'arai!'
meaning——'pain and woe on those I hate'
YOU put him in charge of the *Timoriai*
Enforcers of Your wrath

Sun sings in glory to YOU in priest
:   *'Laïlam'*
in Hebrew with the same name

: anok (I am) :
Bi-ath-yar-ba(r)-ba(r)-ber-birsh—shi   *la-tour-bouf-froum-trom*
(36 letters)

meaning——'I am leading the way for YOU, Lord

ThankYOU I am *Helios* SunDiskgod
getting out of my flat barge'

now in hidden I spell
Your natural name
in Egyptian:
A
l-
d
a-
b
i-
a-
hi
m

(nine letters
going down)

now getting out of Sun's flat barge
wrapping himself in light for eyes is
dogheadfox

he greets YOU with :
'Abrasax = year's number
that's Who YOU are hello'

now leaving the other side of the barge is
sparrow hawk
he greets YOU and
cries for food :

hi   hi   hi   hi   hi   hi   hi   *pippippip*   *pippippip*

Ennead/Company of Nine
say good-day to YOU in priest
'Me-nef-ho-if-hoth'
meaning——they're saying   :
'Lord, I lead the way for YOU'
"

END   PRAYER
****

(break)

then :

   CLAP   *CLAP*   *CLAP*

go ahead
do it

GOD
laughed
seven
(7)
times :

HA   *HA*   *HA*   *HA*   *HA*   *HA*   *HA*
HA   *HA*   *HA*   *HA*   *AH*   *HA*

FROM THE *HIDDEN SACRED BOOK*
OF MOSES CALLED "EIGHTH" OR "HOLY"

Like *GOD|gods,* this is a Greek text written in Egypt probably
by a heterodox Jew. It contains a different version of the tale
of GOD's Seven Laughs, longer than the one found in
GOD|gods. Text: Papyrus XIII in *Papyri Graecae Magicae.*

the 7 Laughs of GOD
Hha   Hha   Hha   Hha   Hha   Hha   Hha

each Laugh HE gave
engendered the 7
god god god god god god god
the Fore-Appearers
who clasp everything one

first Laugh
PHOS(AUGE)   showed up
Light(Flash)

               All splitter
               born universe god
                   fire god

second Laugh
HUDOR filling everywhere
Water

               he echoed
               Earth heard
               she saw AUGE
                   Flash
               she was afraid
               and writhed
        the HUGRON waving tender smooth
           the Wet

GOD cut in threes
        three lots
        three destinies

              a new god took light

              whom GOD arranged
              to rule water's pit

              so unless this god helps

              HUGRON won't grow
              Wet

              bigger or smaller

              tides billow
              and curl up

WaterMaster's
named :

Prom-sach-ha   Al-eh-eh-i-oh

      for you are

O - e - a - i
      be-thel-leh

third Laugh
GOD wanting to

appeared from HIS rage
NOUS(KAI PHRENES)
Mind(and Brains)

given a heart

his name:
Hermes

translates the diacosm's totals
interprets whatever is

in charge of Phrenes
he manages

he is the steward
of universe house

of course he is:
She-meh-shi-lamps

fourth Laugh

apparent self GENNA
                FuckMakeBabies

                        witnessing she is strong
                        over everything's sperm

                        all that's seeded
                        turned a parent

                        thanks her
                        named :

                Ba-day-to-foth   Zoh-thaks-at-hoh-dsoh

fifth Laugh
GOD smiled wept
showed in light MOIRA
                Lot-Portion

                        holding a balance beam

                        meaning in her
                        justice is minded

                        Hermes argued said:
                        "she's got my job"

                        they quarreled
                        GOD came out:

                        "what is right you
                        two bring to light

                        but all in the universe
                        will stand under you"

first to take the scepter
of creation

she is named
in holy

anagrammed
because so
fearful

it makes you
shudder

it is

thaw-ri-ow-bri-tih and so on

(her name in anagram
is bigstrong
holy
all honor it everywhere
yes a much name
strength name:

thaw-ri-ow-bri-tih-tam-mah-ohr-rang-ah-doh-
i-oh-dang-ar-roh-am-mah-tir-boy-roth,

49, letters)

sixth Laugh

made HIMself joyous

KAIROS   turned light
ModeSeason

carried a rod
meaning KingMastery

handed it
to [Phos]
god light
built first

who took it
said:

"let yourself enter
the globe of hoped-for glory
                    of PHOS
                          Light

and be next
        to me
because before anyone else did
you gave me the rod that rules

whatever was
and likely will
you stand over"

after heshe went into the sphere of Light
the SunDisk
who spins in center
around himself
displayed an airbreath of Phos

GOD said to queen [Kairos?]
"all right
be englobed
in that airbreath

stay with Phos
hold everything
in circling embrace

grow through Light
take and stop taking
from him

you help
and whatever is
waxes wanes"

[Kairos'?] bigstrong astonishing name :

"anagh (I am) :
Bi-ath-yar-bar   ber-bish-hi-la   tour   bou-froun-trohm"
                              (36 letters)

seventh Laugh

wheezed while HE did it

bore PSYCHÉ
        SoulBreath

everything got moving

GOD said:

"you'll keep them that way
on the move

and happy
when Hermes gives you the road"

HE stopped talking
they all started moving
each along their road
Living Wind bellying them
and
there's no
stopping them

GOD looked
HE went

        pepepepepepepepepepepepep

                                        just like a bird

startle
scaring everyone

PHOBOS   dressed in light
ScarePanic

full armed armored
god named:

Danoup   Hhrator   Berbalih   Balbithih
                    (26 letters)

then He bowed beckoned to Earth
gave a big

SSHHSSHHSSHHSSHHSSHHSSHHSSHH

snake's tone

she caught HIS note
opened her womb neck
bore special child Pythian Python
who knows about things
                    before they happen
thanks to the piercing snakesound GOD made

Python's big holy name:

Ililloúih

I-lil-lou-ih

I-lil-lou-ih

i-thor

marmaraugeh

foh-hhoh

foh-boch

after Python showed
Earth doubled up
reared up
pranced

Sky Axle held still
although portioned
to come with her
moving his stick
          in her time

GOD said:
        "Yah-Woh!"

everything stopstood

rose in light
[Yah-Woh]
big god biggest
standing things
in the universe
before now
and later

no longer
did any aerial mists
of heavenly lands
get mislaid
out of order
no way

Phobos saw
askedknew:
        "Yah-Woh stronger than me?"

stood against him
butted
"I was here before you"
rebutted
"I stood everything"

GOD said:
"Phobos you are the child
                of a bird call
he of snake hiss
         a better noise
              than made you
yet from you two will come
when you show up later
power to make all things stand
the way they're allotted"

Yah-Woh's named

Danoup   Hhrator   Berbalih   Balbith,   Yah-Woh

GOD chose to offer aslant
honor to the god [Yah-Woh]
                              standing aside with HIM

so when he showed
GOD gave him the nine gods
to lead in front
holding equal
power and glory

HE called their nine distinctions
named the horn tips of their names:
"Bosbeadii"

and the seven planetstars:

a	e	e	i	o	u	o
e	e	i	o	u	o	
e	i	o	u	o		
i	o	u	o			
o	u	o				
u	o					
o						

o	u	o	i	e	e	a
u	o	i	e	e	a	
o	i	e	e	a		
i	e	e	a			
e	e	a				
e	a					
a						

(bigstrong amazing anagram)

biggestbest one's HIS name
that strong one
27 letters

Abohrch   braohch   hhrammaohth   Yah-Woh

putting it another way:

Abrohch   braohch   hhrammaohth   prohap   bathoh
Yah-Woh   o   u   a   e   e   i   o   u   o

FROM THE *POIMANDER*
OF HERMES TRISMEGISTOS

A Greek revision of an earlier Egyptian cosmology, c. A.D. 100.
Text: Nock, trans., Festugière, ed., *Corpus Hermeticum,* Vol. 1,
1–19, 30–31.

One day I started thinking about what was real; my mind had
gone from me to so high a place my senses ceased. Sleep weighed
me down, just as if I had eaten too much or overworked. I
saw a Great Man (how big he was, I couldn't tell, but he was
enormous) coming toward me. He called my name and said:

"What do you want to hear and see? And learn and know
                                                        through thought?"

"Who are you?"

"I am Poimander Men'sShepherd Mind of Authentia Absolute Master.
I know what you want to do. Wherever you are I am."

"I'd like to find out what is real—and how it came to birth.
I want to know god."

"Think. And I will teach you."

then he changed the way I saw him
I looked inside him and found
he'd opened every thing for me to see
in a downward turning.

an infinite vision overcame me
light born(e) wherever I turned
                                        light calm clear laughing gently full
I watched I loved

Afterward I saw the darkness that silts toward the bottom
                                        squatting in her corner
begin raining her somber face
spiraling out like a (snake) sidewinding her coils

                    then she seemed
        to change into a water shaken from within
                from depths beyond telling
then smoke as if she held inside her (unseen) fires
returning echoes trebly pitched chiming notes sadder than words

she screamed what no "a," "an," or "the" could give sense to
hissing and crackling like a voice of fire

out of the light . . .
holy Word plunged into this BirthWorld Darkness

clear fire leapt from Water up into the high
bursting with act
lightly piercing my eye

Air of Light
chased this FireWind
she closed herself up under him
                    mounting above Earth and Water
which makes it seem she hangs onto him

Land and Sea stayed below where they were
mixing/mingling each other
impossible to tell one from the other
stirred by the Wind'sWord born(e) within earshot against them

"Do you know what you saw?"

"I will"

"I am Light your god Mind
who gave myself to sight
before DarkWater's birth
the glowing Word Mindvoiced
is god's son"

"And then?"

"Know
what hears in you and sees
is the Word of the Lord

your mind the FatherGod

Father and Son are One
this makes life

now turn towards the Light
and understand"

he stopped talking and looked me straight in the face for so
long I started shaking. That was when

he raised his head
I saw in my mind
the Light born in countless powers
bear the infinite ordered world

the Fire hemmed in everywhere by the strongest power
still stood in place

all this   in my mind
while I looked inside at the world
through Poimander's Word

I was still lost inside ecstasy
when he spoke again

"you see in your mind the seeming that starts type
beginning the beginning
of the beginning that never stops"

"where did the rows/the L M Nts of birth come from?"

"from god's intention
once it has taken Word
and sees the lovely World of Birth

she remembers to execute by heart
whatever he says
setting herself in order through the rows of birth
and the SoulBreaths, their first yield

god the malefemale Mind Life Light the first being and doing
bore by Word Worker Mind 2 the fire/wind/god
who worked up from scratch seven Comptroller Stars
who fold their circles around the world strained
                                    to human notice
they call their Accounts *Heimarmené* : Lot-Payment

immediately god's Word bounded away
                        from the downward bearing (birth) rows
towards that light-scoured workfact named BirthWorld
making himself one with Worker Mind 2
for they enjoyed the same birth
leaving behind the crazed wordless sloping L M Nts
to furnish unwrought subject things

Worker Mind 2 with Word
enclosed the (Stars') circles
holding on to their buzzing cones
he made these workfacts of himself wheel on their own
                        right from a start without beginning
towards an undetermined end that never stops
for (the Stars') bearings end where they begin
giving birth as willful Mind permits
to the crazed Wordless lives
of those the stooping rows of birth inform

air brings forth those that fly; water those who swim

land and sea split
cutting away from each other differently

the Earth had four-footed and creepingcrawling children
the animals tame and wild

All Father Mind Light and Life
bore Anthropos the Great Man to be his image
whom he fell so deeply in love with
because the childMan was his
Anthropos the Lovely
no matter how you looked at him was
Dad's true mirror

when Mind discovered love outside himself
in fact in his (son's) bodyform
he gave him sovereignty
over all the creatures Worked from Thought

when the Great Man saw
what Worker Mind 2 had done with Fire
he wanted that gift for himself

his Father agreed

Anthropos fathered himself
inside Worker's Sphere
where he was to be absolute lord
the Comptrollers fell in love with him
they gave him each
a share in their power

once he learned who they are
and had enjoyed their birthrights
he wanted to shred their circles' sheltering limit
to find out for himself
how strong he who sits on fire and rules it is

Anthropos
who now held all there is of the appointed world of the dying
of those who live mindless/wordless
cast his bent below (the Stars') harmonious windings
tearing apart their cunted shell
he showed falling BirthWorld god's lovely body

she saw he owned in him beauty
and all the (Stars') energy
while his body formed Fathergod's mirror
she gave him a smile for Eros/Love
for she'd seen her oceans reflect
                              his supreme loveliness
which sometimes shaded her earth

he too had seen her seem
to borrow his shape in the water
and loved her for that
planning to make her house his home
will gave him the strength
to plunge into her silly wordless box
BirthWorld opened taking him in
enlacing her beloved
inside her sheer Wholes
they mixed and mingled
they loved each other

which is why
of all who live on earth
it's only people
who compound twice in doubt

I mean they either die through body
or else live without death
        through Anthropos who appears the way he is

for while everyone is immortal
and has   power over all things
they still suffer death's enclosure
                subjecting themselves to Lot-Portion

and although (born) beyond the Stars' pinched wheels
they enslave themselves making the heavens their Paymaster

once true malefemales
                because their father was
and tireless

because heshe never needed sleep
. . . (they wind up)   defeating themselves"

"I too love Word"

"what I tell now is the Secret hidden until this day

after BirthWorld slept with Anthropos
she did something almost unbelievable

since the Great Man had shared
half by Fire half by WindSoulAir
in the birthrights of the Seven Comptrollers
                        and their fixed symmetry
she did not wait
she immediately sluiced out of her funnels

seven malefemales (moving) high above this world
mockmiming the original Stars"

"more"

"Silence. I have not finished beginning

The first people were born like this
first there was Girl Earth
then FuckFather Water

Fire made them ripen

then BirthWorld took Windsoul(s) from FireAir
and bore bodies that looked like the Great Man's

Anthropos of Life and Light
reproduced himself
changing his Life to Soul
                Light to Mind

34   ORIGINS

staying that way
(he became) every(breathing/thinking) thing
                    in the apparent world
until time closed one cycle
and the moment of birth into species began

listen closely: this is what you've been waiting for

when that moment came around
(Father)God willed the chain that binds one and all
to let go

every living thing that (up till then) was malefemale
untied

dissecting into sex
even the people

some breaking into men
others women

Immediatcly (Father)God spoke to them in holy Word:
'grow in your growings
fill by filling
all of (Worker Mind's) FactMadeThings

be minded
know yourself
            means you will not die

the only way you can do that
is to love

find out about everything that is'

After God spoke his ForeThought
            worked through Lot-Portion
            and the Stars' tightly-meshing wheels
she manipulated the sexes' mingling
building their generations from below

everything prevailed in multiples of kind

all who know they will not die
reach that gentle goodness
        which is everywhere

those who love the body
        the child of vagrant love
remain below and roam the ShadowWorld
        in deep pain
    because death's business
        concludes their sensings"

. . .

this is why I made a song of praise
with all my strength and soul'sbreath
for Father God:
"Blessed is God
        Father of the Wholes
          Whose powers execute his will
          Who wishes to Know
            and be Known by
              His own
        Who gave by Word
             everything that is
           understanding
        Whose image all BirthWorld bore
        Whose body/shape
          she did not change
       Who stronger than His every power
          rules over the high and mighty
        Master of those who praise Him

receive the pure word sacrifices of my soulbreath
        and heart stretched to the limit towards You
      The Uninvocable
      The unnameable
        Spoken-Only-In-Silence"

The cosmogony of the Hebrew P Document, Genesis 1.1–2.4a,
c. 550–450 B.C. Text: Kittel, *Biblia Hebraica.*

At the first of the gods' godmaking skies and earth, the earth was
all mixed up—darkness on top of deepness; so the gods' spirit swooped
down on the waters.

The gods said LIGHT   so there was light, and the gods liked the
light so they made it different from the darkness:

> they called the light Day
> called the darkness Night;

> so that was Evening
> and that was Morning
> the first Day.

Then the gods said, LET A SPACE BE BEATEN OUT,   and
it was TO SPLIT THE WATERS UNDERNEATH IT FROM THE
WATERS ON TOP OF THE SPACE.

> the gods called the space Skies

> so that was evening
> and that was morning
> the second day.

Then the gods said, LET THE WATERS-BENEATH-THE-
SKIES BE GATHERED TOGETHER INTO ONE GROUP SO
THE DRYNESS CAN BE SEEN.

And they were.

> the gods called the dryness land
> called the gathering-together-of-the-waters seas.

> The gods liked what they saw

so they said

> SPROUT THE EARTH SPROUTS:
> GRASS SEEDING SEEDS
> TREES MAKING FRUIT,
> FRUIT ITS SEED IN IT,
> EVERY KIND ON EARTH.

So it was like that; the earth brought out sprouts: kinds of seed
seeding grass, kinds of seed-in-fruit-making trees
               and the gods liked it.

               so that was evening
               and that was morning
               the third day.

Then the gods said, LET THERE BE LIGHTS IN THE SPACE
OF THE SKIES TO SET THE DAY OFF FROM THE NIGHT.
THEY'LL BE MARKING TIMES, DAYS AND YEARS, AND
THEY'LL BE LIGHTS IN THE SKIESPACE LIGHTING THE
EARTH.

So that's how it was: the gods made the two big lights: the
bigger light for running the day and the littler light to run the night
with the stars.

               the gods presented them
               in the skiespace
               to light the earth
               to run day and night
               to make a difference
               between the light and the darkness

               and the gods liked it.

               so that was evening
               and that was morning
               the fourth day.

Then the gods said
               SWARM WATERS SWARMS
               BREATHING LIFE
               AND FLYERS FLYING
               OVER THE EARTH
               OVER CROSS SKIESPACE

so the gods godmade big sea beasts, and all breathing crawling life
on Earth; the waters swarmed and all the birdwing
               and the gods liked it
               and blessed them:

BREED A LOT, AND FILL
THE WATERS OF THE SEAS
AND THE FLYER MAKE MANY
ON THE EARTH.

so that was evening
and that was morning
the fifth day.

Then the gods said, LET THE EARTH BRING OUT
BREATHING LIFE OF ALL SORTS: CATTLE AND
CRAWLER, EVERY EARTH LIFE
and that's how it was:
Gods made all earth life
cattle and red-dirt crawler too
all of all kinds
and liked it
so the gods said
LET'S MAKE SOME RED DIRT THAT'LL
LOOK LIKE US,
JUST LIKE US
IT'LL BOSS:
THE FISH IN THE SEA
THE BIRD IN THE SKY
AND CATTLE
AND ALL THE EARTH
AND ALL THE CRAWLERS CRAWLING
THE EARTH
so the gods
godmade man as he looks
looking like the gods
they godmade them
prick and hole
they godmade them

and the gods blessed them
and the gods said to them:

BREED A LOT AND FILL THE EARTH
AND TAKE IT OVER.
RULE:

THE FISH OF THE SEA
THE FLYER OF THE SKIES
ALL LIFE THAT CRAWLS ON THE EARTH.

Then the gods said
HERE WE'VE GIVEN YOU:
EVERY SEED SEEDING SPROUT
OVER CROSS THE WHOLE EARTH,
EVERY TREE BEARING FRUIT
SEEDING SEED
FOR FOOD,
FOR YOU;

AND FOR EVERY:
LIFE ON EARTH
FLYER OF THE SKIES
CRAWLER ON THE EARTH
BREATHING LIFE,
EVERY GREEN SPROUT
FOR FOOD.
and that's how it was

and the gods liked everything they saw
very much
so that was evening
and that was morning
the sixth day.

Now the skies, earth, and all their troop were complete. The gods
finished off all the work they'd done on the sixth day, and rested on
the seventh day from all the work they'd done.

The gods blessed the seventh day,
set it apart,
because they'd rested on it
after all the works
the gods had godmade to work.

That's the story of the godmaking of the skies and earth

"WISDOM" FROM *ECCLESIASTICUS*

From *Ecclesiasticus*/Ben Sira, a Hebrew text of the second or
third century B.C., Pharisaic. Texts: Vulgate, Septuagint, Levi—
The Hebrew Text of the Book of Ecclesiasticus. Ecclesiasticus
24.3–12a.

(Wisdom speaks of herself)

"I came out of El's mouth   first
    flooded across the earth
then built my home high
            my seat in cloud pillar

I was alone   traveling the circle of Sky
            going back and forth through Tehom-deeps

I held seawave and all the earth
        every people and nation

                        seeking rest with all
'Whose home can I stay in?'

The One who made everything assigned me
The One who made me set my stay:
                        said
'Stay with Jacob
Set yourself in Jerusalem'

He made me   starting   before the world
I do not stop   ever
I served in the Tent
then set in the Temple
I stayed in the Holy City
            the power of Jerusalem
I rooted in the Chosen People"

THE SEVEN DAYS OF GENESIS
FROM THE *SECRETS OF ENOCH*

From *The Book of the Secrets of Enoch,* a Hebrew-Greek-Slavonic text, c. first century B.C. Text: Charles and Morfill, *The Book of the Secrets of Enoch.* "(*B:* . . .)" indicates alternate readings from B version; "(. . .)" indicates suppositions; "(. . . ?)" indicates guesses; "???" indicates lost words; "***" indicates approximate sense, syntax corrupt.

God speaks to Enoch face to face

"Enoch—sit beside me
on my left with Gabriel"
I knelt in front of him

"Enoch whom I love—
I tell you that
everything you see
that stands complete
from before it began
I made (taking)
all that you see
from what you do not
from that which is not

hear what I have not told
my angels who don't know
how they began or why
my kingdom never ends

who haven't heard
how I opened light
and rode inside
like a ghost
like Sun when he visits east to west
yet lives in peace with himself

for I did not
when doing everything
I conceived the thought of creation
putting a floor under it
letting everyone see
what I had done
the bottom of dark

I called down to the deep below
'come from the unseen dark
all that eye can see
Adoïl—come'

he came hauling so large
a stone of light it made
his belly a giant ball

'explode—Adoïl
push out the light
give it birth'

he blew out the stone
light gaping his belly womb
opening all I willed for shape

light the mother of light
bore a great age
the star heaven
which I saw was good

(where)
I built a chair
and sat down

then :
'light—rise
above my throne
take body as home
for the highest (stars)'

I leaned back on my seat
and looked up
above light
there is nothing

the bottom once more

again I called
to the darkness you cannot see
'come—Archas
heavy stiff and deeply red (*B:* black)
tear bright firm body
from the unseen (wavering dark?)'

he lived up to my word

'Archas—undo (your belly womb)'

he shook loose from his hollows
(earth realm)
an age I saw was good
big black mother
rearing the make
of all who live in her

'Archas—go down (to her)
house in your body
the lower world'

which he did

(under Archas)
below dark
there is nothing

water circled with light planted on seven islands

I said
'???—come from light and dark
thicken shape'

and ??? happened

which I layered in sheets with light
and set down for a road

this is how water
a path below light
spread over shadow
was born

bottomless water
who I made take body

who I embraced in seven glowing disks
(one inside the other)
working in concentrics
outward towards the last

who I drew of such crystal
that is wet and dry
glass pictures it

every root I showed a path
water I told
'ebb and flow
your way'

I set the seven stars
in the sky each a track

all this
I saw was good

light and dark
scampering in water
I made differ—
to the light
'you are day'
to the dark
I said
'you are night'

evening and morning : the first day

the week of God
his wisdom and power every moment all those seven days
the strengths of sky earth's might
everything that moves
meaning men and women too

into the sky's disk
I put body
water I compelled into one
draining the confusion between wet and not-wet
the big rocks grown from water
I heaped up
I cut of fire
ten squads of immaterial stars
my angels Cherubim Seraphim Ophannim (etc.)
who dress in
whose weapons are flame
my advice to them
'each one
keep to your ranks'

Satanaïl and his angels thrown down from the high place

one did not
he turned away
taking his band

he mothered a thought without force (or: that could never reach act) :
to lift his chair above the clouds sheathing earth
equating himself to me

I threw him down

Satanaïl flew through the air
above the abyss
and didn't stop

(evening and morning :)

the third day

before starting the living
and feeding them
I said to earth
'grow trees big with fruit
shoot up grass hills
and every seed for sowing'

I planted Paradise Park
and walled it off
armed fire angels
standing guard

I made earth spring
and gave her this law
'do it over and over again'

evening and morning :

the fourth day

I ordered fires (for the cone)
of the sky's circles

for the first and highest : the (biggest) stars (and)
                              Kruno (Kronos/Saturn)
for the second : Aphrodit (Venus)
the third : Aris (Ares/Mars)
(? the fourth : ???)
fifth : Zeus (Jupiter)
sixth : Ermis (Hermes/Mercury)
seventh and lowest : Moon ordering her way
                     elegantly with the smallest stars

in the bottom ring
I stationed Sun
to light up day
Moon and (smallest?) stars
to provide for night

my orders for the sun
'journey with each zodiac beast
until (you've matched with all) twelve'

I told month
to follow month
until (they'd reached) twelve
I gave them
names lives thunder-seasons
marked hours
drew lines
for them

evening and morning :

the fifth day

I said to the sea
'make the kinds you can
of fish
of bird of feather
all who creep
and walk on earth
who fly through air
(sex them)
male and female
every soul drawing life's breath

(*B:* then I told [Achamoth] my Wisdom
to make man for me)

evening and morning :

the sixth day

I told (Achamoth) my Wisdom
'give me a male-sex man
of seven standings :
of flesh of earth
blood of rain
eyes sun
bones rock
mind from angels' wing and speeding cloud
veins (nails?) hair earth's grass
soul my breath and wind'

I said to (new-made) man
'what you can do
makes seven :
flesh hears
eye sees
soul scents

veins touch
blood tastes
you are boned
so be strong
find sweet joy
through mind'

this is the puzzle for him
in words I set that day :
'man held of what he does and does not see
lives and dies
figure him out'

*** little in his bigness
big in his littleness
speaks as well as
any I made ***

my second angel
of honor and glory

king of the world
sharing (Achamoth) my Wisdom

I made earth
his house
where none of all
I made who are
is his like

from the four hinges
(joining the lands' orb)
that also name
the four stars
I set for him
(Antolia [rising/East]
  Dysis [setting/East]
  Arctos [the Bear/North]
  Mesembria [mezzogiorno/South])
I called him Adam (Tetragrammaton)

I showed him
the two roads
of light and dark
'light is good
dark evil
I will find out
if you love
or hate me
if any of you
really do

what you do not
I know
who you are
you are ignorant of—so
you will go worse wrong
death follows sin'

I made him sleep
(his last word awake
was 'mother')
I took one of his ribs
and fleshed woman
for him to die through
I called her 'mother'
his last word 'Eve'

Paradise Park the sky opening the angels' victory song

Adam lived on earth
(where) I built (him) a garden
in the East in Eden
so he would obey my laws
and keep my word

I took the top off sky
he saw my angels
sing victory

Adam lived in the Garden
never leaving

the devil knew what I wanted
to make another world
because Adam ruled (this one)

devil : evil bottom agent

*** as a runaway he made
he made Sotona of sky ***

because he is called Satomaïl
he grew away from the angels
but what he is does not break his mind
he can still tell right from wrong
he knows why I threw him down
what he had done for me to do that

which is why he hated Adam
as thought he went between Eve's legs
without touching him

I curse ignorance
all I promised life
I do not turn from
and blight
I did not spoil man earth
or whatever else I did

I do damn his fruit
when it is rotten
when what he does
(brings on darkness)

rebel Adam driven out
God's desire not to destroy him
for all the years that will be

I said to him
'you are earth
back to the earth
I raised you from

I will not unmake you
but send you back
to the house of your birth
I promised life
to all I made
whether you see it or not'

Adam lived five and half hours
in Paradise

I blessed Sabbath
the seventh day
when people stop

the age of the world :

seven thousand years
the eighth thousandth ends
not years months weeks days

I drew up the eighth day
the first-made
after my creation

this is why
the first seven days (of the world)
return to figure
the first seven thousand years

when year eight thousand starts
time stops ending and rests
free from years months weeks days hours"

TWO STORIES FROM EZRA
THE APOCALYPTIST

A Latin text, c. third or fourth century A.D., from a Greek original, c. second century A.D. Text: Bensley, *The Fourth Book of Ezra*, in Robinson, ed., *Texts and Studies*, Vol. III.

1.

I said

    Lord—if I have (ever) found grace before your eyes
    reveal to your slave through whom you visit your creation

he said

        the beginning of the Sphere of Earth
        before the exits of time
        before the conventicles of wind
        before the voice of thunder
        before the lightning flash
        before elegant flowers
        before strengthening the powers of going
        before gathering uncounted troupes of Messengers
        before lifting up the heights of air
        before naming the measures of sky fixed above Earth
        before reckoning the worth of the footstool of Zion
        before numbering the present
        before sweeping away the inventions
                of those who sin now
                and sealing those who keep
                the treasury of faith
     I thought
     I did
        and no one else

I said

>>what will be the separation of time?
>>when will be the end of that that was?
>>>>the beginning of that that is to follow?

he said

>>from Abraham to Abraham
>>from him Jacob and Esau
>>he held Jacob's hand
>>>>he held Esau's foot
>>>>from the beginning
>>Esau ends today
>>Jacob begins tomorrow
>>. . . the hand of a man . . .
>>between the heel and the hand
>>look for nothing else
>>Ezra

2.

I said

>>Lord—speaking you told me of the beginning of creation
>>you said "let sky and earth be done"

>>>>and your word did

>>>>wind flying
>>>>shadow surrounding
>>>>silence

>>>>man's voice not sounding in front of you
>>>>>>not yet

>>you said "take a light from my light"
>>>>>>take it from my treasuries
>>>>>>to make my work seen

on the second day you made Wind of the sky fixed above Earth
you told him to divide
he divided Water
he made her go up in part
part he made stay below

on the third day you told Water to assemble
on 1/7 of Earth
you dried out 6/7 of Earth
saving her
to be planted and sown
to give you food and drink
out in the open

your word went out
the deed was done

there came
the fruit of endless abundance
in desire of taste in many forms
and flowers of colors we cannot do
and perfumes of scents we cannot find

on the fourth day you ordered sun's splendor moon's glow
stars spread out
you said
"wait on man"

on the fifth day you told the 1/7 where Water was assembled
to make the birds and fish

Water (who) had become silent and breathless
made them as you told her to
so that the peoples would talk of your wonderful deeds
you saved two
whom you called Behemoth and Leviathan
you separated them from each other

the 1/7 where Water was assembled could not hold them
you gave Behemoth the 1/7
which was dried out on the third day
to live where there are 1,000 hills

you gave Leviathan the 1/7 of Water

you saved them to feed those you want and when

on the sixth day you told Earth to make out in the open
the beasts of burden
the wild animals
and snakes

you made Adam lead everything you made

THE *SEFER YETZIRA*

The Book of Creation (Sefer Yetzira), a Hebrew text of the
mystic tradition (Neo-Pythagorean), c. third–sixth centuries
A.D. Text: The four texts in *Sefer Yetzira*, Lewin-Epstein
Publishers, Jerusalem, 1965.

With 32 wondrous ways of wisdom

> YAH
> YHVH TSEVA'OT   (OF HOSTS)
> ELOHEI YISRAEL   (GOD OF ISRAEL)
> ELOHIM ḤAYIM   (LIVING GOD)
> EL SHADAI   (OMNIPOTENT GOD)
> RAM VE-NISA'   (RAISED HIGH)
> SHOKHEN 'AD   (ETERNAL DWELLER)

His Name high and holy

carved, covenanted,
drilled, and created his world,

through three Sefarim:

> Sefer   (book)=writing
> Sfor   (counting)=number
> Sippur   (telling)=speech

Ten Sefirot (numbers) made of Nothingness
Twenty-two Foundation Letters

Ten Sefirot as the number of the ten fingers
5 paralleling 5
    the Covenant set in the middle
the way the tongue makes the word   the Naked Word

Ten Sefirot of Nothingness   Ten and not Nine   Ten and not Eleven
    Understand this wisely   Search it out intelligently

    Measure with them   Search out from them

Know and consider   then Be Silent:

Set the Word at its Origin & return the Maker to His Place

For He is the Maker   creating alone   He has no peer
and Their number is Ten   and They have no end

Ten Sefirot made of Nothing
                    Brake your heart from thinking too quickly
                    Brake your mouth from speaking

                    If your heart races ahead
                    return
                    for it is said
                    "the creatures ran and returned"

                    The Covenant was made for this

Ten Sefirot made of Nothing
                    Their end is lodged in Their beginning
                    Their beginning in Their end
                    a flame and a coal

                    Know
                    then consider then Be silent:
                    that the Lord is unique
                    the Maker is one
                    He has no peer.

                    What number comes before One?

Ten Sefirot made of Nothing
                    Their number is Ten   and They have no end

                    The range of beginning
                    the range of end

                    The range of good
                    the range of evil

                    The range of height
                    the range of depth

The range of east
the range of west

The range of north
the range of south

Only Lord
God Faithful King
Patent of all
from the Residence of His Holiness to Eternity

Ten Sefirot made of Nothing
           Their appearance is the look of lightning
           Their disappearance: They have no end

           His Word is in them as they come and go
           At His command They race like the whirlwind
           and bow before His throne

Ten Sefirot made of Nothing
Twenty-two Foundation Letters
Three Mothers
Seven Doubles
Twelve Simples

The Spiritwind in each of them

Ten Sefirot made of Nothing
           The first: The Spiritwind of Living God
       His throne set from the beginning
       Blessed the Name of Eternal Life   forever continually
       Voice   and Spiritwind   and Speech

       The Speech   the Holy Spiritwind
       Origin without beginning
       End beyond ending

Ten Sefirot made of Nothing
                    The first: The Spiritwind of Living God

                    The second: Wind from the Spiritwind

                    The third: Water from the Wind

                    The fourth: Fire from the Water
                              and height and depth
                              and East and West
                              and North and South

The second: Wind from the Spiritwind
                    He carved and lawed by them:
              the four winds of the skies
              East and West
              North and South

              The Spiritwind in each of them

The third: Water from Wind
                    He carved and lawed by them:
              Tohu and Bohu
              Mud and Clay

              He made them a garden
              Set them a wall
              Roofed them with plaster
              Poured snow upon them   and it became dust
              as it is said:
              "He said to the snow 'Be earth' "

              Tohu a green line which surrounds the world
              Bohu stones leveled and sunk in the Deep
              water comes out from between them

The fourth: Fire from Water

He carved and lawed by it:
Glory Throne
Serafim
Ofanim
Creatures of Holy   they are the
Serving Angels

From the three of them He founded His place
as it is said:
"He makes His angels spiritwinds
          His servants a flaming fire"

The fifth: Sealed the height
          He chose three of the Simple letters
          fixed them by His Great Name YHV
          sealed by them the six directions:

    He turned Up   Sealed it by HYV

The sixth: Sealed the under
          He turned Below   Sealed it by YVH

The seventh: Sealed east
          Turned before   Sealed it by VYH

The eighth: Sealed west
          Turned behind   Sealed it by VHY

The ninth: Sealed south
          Turned right   Sealed it by YHV

The tenth: Sealed north
          Turned left   Sealed it by HVY

These are the ten Sefirot made of Nothing:

The first: The Spiritwind of Living God

The second: Wind from the Spiritwind

The third: Water from the Wind

The fourth: Fire from the Water

and height
and depth
and East
and West
and North
and South

Twenty-two Foundation Letters
Three Mothers
Seven Doubles
Twelve Simples

All of   them are Lawed by the voice
                Carved by the breathwind
                Fixed by the mouth at five places

ALEF   ḤET   HE   'AYIN

GIMEL YOD   KAF   KUF

DALET   TET   LAMED   NUN   TAV

ZAYIN   SAMEKH   TZADI   RESH   SHIN

BET   VAV   MEM   PE

as much a part of the tongue they are as a flame and a coal

ALEF   ḤET   HE   'AYIN   made where the end of the tongue
                                    comes against the throat

BET   VAV   MEM   PE   between the lips
                              at the head of the tongue

GIMEL YOD   KAF   KUF   on the back third
                                    of a divided tongue

DALET TET LAMED NUN TAV   the head of the tongue
made by the voice

ZAYIN SAMEKH TZADI RESH SHIN   between the teeth
the tongue low and flat

Twenty-two Foundation Letters
fixed on the wheel at 231 Gates
the wheel turns forward and back

The mark of a thing/word:
if good   nothing is greater than happiness
if evil   nothing is worse than torture

Twenty-two letters He:
>   Lawed
>   Carved
>   Weighed
>   Combined
>   ALEF with all of them
>   Combined them and made
>   the soul of all made things
>   and the soul of all things to be made

How did He weigh them and combine them?

>   ALEF with all of them
>   all with ALEF
>
>   BET with all of them
>   all with BET
>
>   and so with all of them
>   returning empty
>   going out from the 231 Gates
>   so that all the souls of all made things
>   and all speech
>   comes out of one Name

He made the Distinct from the Indistinct
    made the Nothing Something
    carved great rocks from the air that has no substance

The three Mothers   ALEF   MEM   SHIN
are like a scales   one plate for what is earned
                        one for what is owed

                        the tongue of law keeps them apart

The three Mothers ALEF   MEM   SHIN
are a great secret
covered   wondrous   hidden   by six rings
Fire   Water and Wind come out of them
dividing into male and female

Know   Consider   and Be Silent
Fire bears Water

The three Mothers   ALEF   MEM   SHIN
the birth of the sky is from fire
the birth of the air is from wind
the birth of the earth is from water

Fire above   water beneath
the tongue of law keeps them apart

From them Fathers were born
and from them All was made

The three Mothers   ALEF   MEM   SHIN
are   in the world   Wind   Water   and Fire
        the sky made from Fire
        the earth from Water
        the air from Wind keeps them apart

The three Mothers   ALEF   MEM   SHIN
are   in the year   heat   cold   and wet

```
heat    made from Fire
cold    made from Water
wet     made from Wind    keeps them apart
```

The three Mothers ALEF MEM SHIN
are   in the being head   belly   and organ
    the head made from Fire
    the belly made from Water
    the organ made from Wind keeping them apart

The three Mothers ALEF MEM SHIN
He lawed them
    carved them
    combined them
    sealed by them

The three Mothers ALEF MEM SHIN
are in the world

The three Mothers ALEF MEM SHIN
are in the year

The three Mothers ALEF MEM SHIN
are in the being   male and female

He made the letter ALEF king in the air   crowned it   (='avir)
    combined the letters one with another
    made by it:
            air   in the world
            wet   in the year
            organ   in the living being   male and female

He made the letter MEM king in the water   (=mayim)
    crowned it
    combined the letters one with another
    made by it:

```
            earth   in the world
            cold    in the year
            belly   in the living being    male and female
```

He made the letter SHIN king in fire   (=*'esh*)
   crowned it
   combined the letters one with another
   made by it:
```
            sky     in the world
            heat    in the year
            head    in the living being    male and female
```

How did He combine them?
```
                    ALEF  MEM   SHIN
                    ALEF  SHIN  MEM
                    MEM   ALEF  SHIN
                    MEM   SHIN  ALEF
                    SHIN  ALEF  MEM
                    SHIN  MEM   ALEF
```

```
        Sky=Fire        Man's head=Fire
        Air=Wind        Man's belly=Water
        Earth=Water     Man's heart=Wind
```

The three Mothers ALEF   MEM   SHIN
                                                   made with
ALEF   Wind   Air   Wet   Organ   lawed Tongue between

                                                   made with
MEM   Water   Earth   Cold   Belly   plate for what is owned

                                                   made with
SHIN   Fire   Sky   Heat   Head   plate for what is owed

        These are ALEF   MEM   SHIN

The seven Doubles BET GIMEL DALET KAF PE RESH TAV

Founded in Life Peace Wisdom and Richness and Progeny
        and Favor   and Governance

                                                    behave
in double utterance   realized in double:

   BET/VET   GGIMEL/GIMEL   DDALET/DALET
   KAF/KHAF PE/FE   RRESH/RESH   TTAV/TAV
a soft and a hard form   a hero and a weakling

These are the doubles:
                Wisdom/Folly   Richness/Poverty
                Progeny/Barrenness   Life/Death
                Governance/Slavery   Peace/War
                Favor/Ugliness

The seven Doubles BET GIMEL DALET KAF PE RESH TAV
Seven and not six
Seven and not eight
Six sides and six chambers of the Temple
the Holy Palace set in the middle

                Blessed the Glory of God in His Place
                He is the Place of the world
                The world is not his Place
                He bears it all

Seven Doubles BET GIMEL DALET KAF PE RESH TAV
                        of Foundation
He lawed them
He carved them
He combined them
He weighed them
He exchanged them
He made by them: the seven stars of the world
                        the seven days of the year
                        the seven gates of the soul

                        seven and seven

How did he join them?

> Two stones building two houses
> Three stones building six houses
> Four stones building twenty-four houses
> Five stones
> building one hundred and twenty houses
> Six stones
> building seven hundred and twenty houses
> Seven stones
> building five thousand and forty houses
>
> from this point on you must go
>   and think upon
> what the mouth cannot say
> and   the ear cannot hear

He made the letter BET king in Wisdom
    crowned it
    combined it with the others
    made from it:

        Saturn   in the world
        Sabbath   in the year
        Mouth   in the being
                male and female

He made the letter GIMEL king in Richness
    crowned it
    combined it with the others
    made from it:

        Jupiter   in the world
        Sunday   in the year
        The Right Eye   in the being
                male and female

He made the letter DALET king in Progeny
    crowned it
    combined it with the others
    made from it:

                    Mars   in the world
                    Monday   in the year
                    The Left Eye   in the being
                                        male and female

He made the letter KAF king in Life
    crowned it
    combined it with the others
    made from it:
                    Sun   in the world
                    Tuesday   in the year
                    The Right Nostril   in the being
                                        male and female

He made the letter PE king in Governance
    crowned it
    combined it with the others
    made from it:
                    Venus   in the world
                    Wednesday in the year
                    The Left Nostril   in the being
                                        male and female

He made the letter RESH king in Peace
    crowned it
    combined it with the other letters
    made from it:
                    Mercury   in the world
                    Thursday   in the year
                    The Right Ear   in the being
                                        male and female

He made the letter TAV king in Favor
    crowned it
    combined it with the other letters
    made from it:

                    Moon   in the world
                    Friday   in the year
                    The Left Ear   in the being
                                        male and female

By them he carved out:
                    Seven Heavens
                    Seven Earths
                    Seven Seas
                    Seven Rivers
                    Seven Deserts
                    Seven Days
                    Seven Weeks
                    Seven Years
                    Seven Sabbatical Years
                    Seven Jubilees

                    The Holy Palace therefore he carved
as the seventh of every desire beneath the skies

Seven stars in the world:
                    Saturn
                    Jupiter
                    Mars
                    Sun
                    Venus
                    Mercury
                    Moon

Seven days in the year:
                    The seven days of the week

Seven gates in the being   male and female:

Two eyes
Two ears
Two nostrils
the mouth

Seven Heavens:

Vilon	(Curtain)
Raki'a'	(Divider)
Shehakim	(Clouded Heaven)
Zevul	(Dwelling)
Ma'on	(Habitation)
Makhon	(Establishment)
'Aravot	(Hidden Clouds)

Seven earths:

'Adama	(Manearth)
Tevel	(Vegetative earth)
Neshiya	(Underworld)
Tziya	(Desert earth)
Heled	(Dust earth)
'Eretz	(Earth)
Gai'	(Valley)

Each one He made unto itself:

The world to itself
The being to itself
The year to itself

Seven Doubles BET GIMEL DALET KAF PE RESH TAV

made by

BET: Saturn Sabbath and Mouth Life Death

made by

GIMEL: Jupiter Sunday Right Eye Peace Evil

made by

DALET: Mars Monday Left Eye Wisdom Folly

                                                           made by
KAF: Sun Tuesday Right Nostril Richness Poverty

                                                           made by
PE: Venus Wednesday Left Nostril Progeny Barrenness

                                                           made by
RESH: Mercury Thursday Right Ear Favor Ugliness

                                                           made by
TAV: Moon Friday Left Ear Governance Slavery

    These are BET GIMEL DALET KAF PE RESH TAV

Twelve Simples: HE VAV ZAYIN ḤET TET YOD LAMED
                 NUN SAMEKH 'AYIN TZADI KUF

Their Foundation: Twelve   not eleven   Twelve   not thirteen

Twelve
Their Foundation: Seeing Hearing Smelling Talking Tasting
                  Sexual intercourse Movement Anger Laughter
                  Thought Doing Sleep

Twelve slant directions divided into six groups
                 separating wind from wind:

    The Up-East line   The North-East line   The Down-East line
    The Up-South line   The South-East line   The Down-South line
    The Up-West line   The South-West line   The Down-West line
    The Up-North line   The North-East line   The Down-North line

Spreading   Spreading   to Eternity forever
They are the very arms of the world

Twelve Simples: HE VAV ZAYIN ḤET TET YOD LAMED
                 NUN SAMEKH 'AYIN TZADI KUF
He lawed them
   carved them
   combined them
   weighed them
   exchanged them
   made by them:

The Twelve Constellations   in the world
The Twelve Months   in the year
The Twelve Media   in the being
                        male and female

two of them Joying   two of them Slandering
two of them Instructive   two of them Rejoicing
two of them Tearing   two of them Chasing

the stomach and the spleen   the gall and the liver
the kidneys   the gullet and the anus
the hands   the feet
                   He set them up as a sort of
battle line   one across from the other:

They stand in groups of Three:
                  Each one by itself
                  One accusing
                  One defending
                  One separating these two

They stand in groups of Seven:
                  Three against Three
                  One separating these two

Twelve in battle order:
                  Three loving
                  Three warring
                  Three giving life
                  Three killing

Three loving:
                  Heart
                  Ears
                  Eyes

Three hating:
                  Liver
                  Gall
                  Tongue

Three giving life:

> Nostril
> Nostril
> Spleen

Three killing:

> Gullet
> Anus
> Mouth

> God Faithful King governs all of them
> from His Place of Glory to the End of Eternity

One on three
Three on seven
Seven on Twelve
all devoted to each other: A proof of the matter:
> Twenty-two desires   One body

How did he join them?

He made the letter HE king in Speech
   crowned it
   combined it with the others
   made by it:

> Aries   in the world
> Nisan   in the year
> Liver   in the being   male and female

He made the letter VAV king in Thought
   crowned it
   combined it with the others
   made by it:

> Taurus   in the world
> 'Iyar   in the year
> Spleen   in the being   male and female

He made the letter ZAYIN king in Movement
   crowned it
   combined it with the others
   made by it:

Gemini	in the world	
Sivan	in the year	
Gall	in the being	male and female

He made the letter ḤET king in Seeing
   crowned it
   combined it with the others
   made by it:

Cancer	in the world	
Tamuz	in the year	
Stomach	in the being	male and female

He made the letter TET king in Hearing
   crowned it
   combined it with the others
   made by it:

Leo	in the world	
'Av	in the year	
Right Kidney	in the being	male and female

He made the letter YOD king in Doing
   crowned it
   combined it with the others
   made by it:

Virgo	in the world	
'Elul	in the year	
Left Kidney	in the being	male and female

He made the letter LAMED king in Sexual Intercourse
   crowned it
   combined it with the others
   made by it:

Libra	in the world	
Tishrei	in the year	
Anus	in the being	male and female

He made the letter NUN king in Smelling
   crowned it
   combined it with the others
   made by it:

Scorpio	in the world	
Marḥeshvan	in the year	
Gullet	in the being	male and female

He made the letter SAMEKH king in Sleep
   crowned it
   combined it with the others
   made by it:

Sagittarius	in the world	
Kislev	in the year	
Right Hand	in the being	male and female

He made the letter 'AYIN king in Anger
   crowned it
   combined it with the others
   made by it:

Capricorn	in the world	
Tevet	in the year	
Left Hand	in the being	male and female

He made the letter TZADI king in Taste
   crowned it
   combined it with the others
   made by it:

Aquarius	in the world	
Shevat	in the year	
Right Leg	in the being	male and female

He made the letter KUF king in Laughter
    crowned it
    combined it with the others
    made by it:

Pisces	in the world	
'Adar	in the year	
Left Leg	in the being	male and female

He divided them into groups   set them apart   each to itself
the world   to itself   the year   to itself
                    the being   to itself   male and female

Twelve Simples: HE VAV ZAYIN ḤET TET YOD LAMED
                NUN SAMEKH 'AYIN TZADI KUF

                                                    made by
HE   Aries Nisan Liver Seeing Blindness

                                                    made by
VAV   Taurus 'Iyar Spleen Hearing Deafness

                                                    made by
ZAYIN Gemini Sivan Gall Smelling Anosmia

                                                    made by
ḤET   Cancer Tamuz Stomach Speaking Dumbness

                                                    made by
TET   Leo 'Av Right Kidney Tasting Hunger

                                                    made by
YOD   Virgo 'Elul Left Kidney Doing Handicap

                                                    made by
LAMED Libra Tishrei Anus Coition Impotence

                                                    made by
NUN   Scorpio Marḥeshvan Gullet Movement Lameness

					made by
SAMEKH	Sagittarius	Kislev	Right Hand	Anger	Liver ailment

					made by
'AYIN	Capricorn	Tevet	Left Hand	Laughter	Gall ailment

					made by
TZADI	Aquarius	Shevat	Right Leg	Thought	Heart ailment

					made by
KUF	Pisces	'Adar	Left Leg	Sleep	Waking

These are the Simples

HE VAV ZAYIN ḤET TET YOD LAMED
NUN SAMEKH 'AYIN TZADI KUF

All of them sharing   as in a quiver   or a wheel   or the heart

Three Mothers	ALEF MEM SHIN
Seven Doubles	BET GIMEL DALET KAF PE RESH TAV
Twelve Simples	HE VAV ZAYIN ḤET TET YOD LAMED
	NUN SAMEKH 'AYIN TZADI KUF

Three fathers and their progeny   Seven planets and their attendants
Twelve slant directions

Every desire   one against another   God made:
Good   over against   Bad   Bad over against Good
Good   from Good   Bad   from   Bad
Good   makes Bad distinct   Bad   makes Good distinct
Good   kept for the goodly   Bad   kept for the evil

. . .

Part Two

Elemental Creation

I. RISING

A RITUAL FOR THE PURIFICATION
OF A TEMPLE

A Sumero-Akkadian text, this is an important bridge piece connecting these diverse peoples (cp. relevant passages in the Sumerian *Enki and Ninhursag* and *The Deluge* with the Akkadian *Enuma eliš*). Text: F. Thureau-Dangin, *Rituels accadiens*.

Bright house   god house   holy place   not yet
no reed up   no tree made
no brick down   no house up
no house up   no city set
no city set   no being being

no Nippur set   no Ekur built
no Uruk made   no Eana built

no Apsu-house built   no Eridu built

no place   for the bright house   the god house   made

no land   sea

motion in sea cunt

Eridu made   Ešagil rising
Lugaldukuda stays   in Ešagil   in sea cunt
Babylon city built   Ešagil complete

Marduk made pure city   heart's love
for the Igigi   highest   they call it

Marduk sets reed on water
shapes dust   pours around reed
shapes man   for god rest   in house of heart's love

goddess Aruru makes man seed   with him
he shapes animals   and other life of field

he makes Tigris and Euphrates   sets them in their place
he calls their name in fortune
he makes grass   swamp weed   reed   forest
wild green plant   land   bog   swamp
wild cow   calf   ewe   and lamb domesticate
tree-gardens   forests
ram   and mountain goat

Bel Marduk   builds a dam   for the sea
shapes reeds   makes trees
sets bricks   raises buildings
makes houses   builds cities
beings being he made   in cities he made
he makes Nippur   builds Ekur
     makes Uruk   builds Eana

FROM THE PAPYRUS BREMNER-RHIND

This creation text from the Papyrus Bremner-Rhind contains material dating back to c. 2300 B.C. Text: Wallis-Budge, *The Gods of the Egyptians.*

the book of finding out the turnings of {RA
                                       {sun disc lord
and overthrowing {APOPHIS
                      {water snake

say these words
Ra said
after he was {KHEPERA
                {beetle life maker

:

"I am who was Khepera
in the body of Khepera/dung beetle rolling the shitball sun
I turned Khepera
whowhich made everything that came into me

after I became Khepera
many others did too
walking out of my mouth

there was no beetle sky lady Nut
no beetle earth
no earth things lifting off the land
or animals creeping there

I lifted them up/right armhand doing it
out of {NUN
        {the layered waters of the deep
where they were not busy
where my feet could not stand

so I charmed my heart to advantage
built the platform of the world in ⎰MAA
⎱truth straightness

I gave each characteristics
my right eye seeing/doing

I was all alone
⎰SHU   not spat from my mouth
⎱daddy airs
or ⎰TEFNUT   like barley from the earth
   ⎱ma waters

no one else lived in beetle
whose right eye saw/did with mine

I made a platform in my heart talking it into act
there came
the many living things
that came into beetle
children into beetle life
and their children
from birth
from the living things came into beetle
from their births
from their children's children's beetle bodies

yes I
it was me
grabbed my cock
drained seedwater
through my fist back into me
I wrapped myself around cock
joined   in fucking my shadow
fanning me under his cloud
I rained seedwater
spewing it like barley from the earth
into my mouth my own

I sprouted back windman Shu
I dropped raingirl Tefnut

my father {NUN   cared for them
             sky water deep
my right eye which sees/does
right behind them
from the time they walked from me

after I turned beetle god one and lonely god
three came out of my mouth into Khepera
also gods but later than I in this earth
while Shu and Tefnut
raised up out of limp water
found their happiness in Nun

in their following
they brought me
my busy right eye
I tied it to all of my flesh parts back to my heart
and wept [*remit*] over them
that's how people [*romet*] came to life in Khepera
men and women
from the tears pouring from the box of my true right eye

who was angry taking a stick against me
after he'd walked up and found
I'd made another
a false one
to take his place
I gave him fame gave him splendid acts
glories I'd made for myself

so he had to resume his way in the right socket of my face
later to rule this earth far as it is wide
his anger fell away
I gave him what had been lost

I raced up through the plant roots
through everything that snakes along
into all who live in Khepera

god lords Shu and Tefnut
had the children ⎰GEB   and ⎰NUT
                      ⎱Earth   ⎱Sky

god lords Geb and Nut
had the children
Osiris
Horus Khenti-en-irti
Seth
Isis
Nephthys
from the body of their womb
one after the other
they did so
they split themselves into children
in this earth"

FROM THE EGYPTIAN *BOOK OF THE DEAD*

A creation text from the Egyptian *Book of the Dead,* c. 2000–
1500 B.C. Text: Wallis-Budge, *The Egyptian Book of the Dead.*
"/. . ./" denotes explanations; "(. . .)" denotes hieroglyphs.

I am　(bowl　lord all　fluid　owl) ATUM　completing-rising
　　　　　　　　　　of all
the only one
in Nun /chaos-fluid/

I am RA
　(sitting hawk-head　resting　cobra-cock circling SunDisk)
　in first (lotus　papyrus acres　starting up　Horushawk　handgiving)
　　　　I ruled this
he did

Who is he?
Is RA
　　　in first
　　　　when he rose (sun bursting over landline　two arms giving)
　　　in Shu /town/ (as king sat　spoke sealines and ground apart)

　　　before the pillars (more than three　under NUT /sky woman/)
　　　　　　of Shu were
when RA was
　　　　　　upon
the high land of
　　　　　　　Khemennu /Hermopolis–Thothtown/ (eight gods)

I am
the god
the great
who lived
into life by myself (snakebody)
　　　　　　　　　NUN

who lifted clear　speaking
　　　　　　his own name:

"Paut neteru" /company of nine gods/

as god

Who is he then?

He is RA   naming   his flesh pieces

are   young   alive

as gods who are the standing feet of RA

I am
without anything giving repulse
in gods

Who is he then?
ATUM he is
in his SunDisk
RA
in rising   going out
in the eastern line of heaven

I am
yesterday
know
tomorrow

Who is he then?

Yesterday OSIRIS (a throne above the Horuseye   a seated god)
Tomorrow
the day his enemies
enemies of NEBERTCHER
    (all lord   open mouth   bound offering   seated god) /OSIRIS/
are destroyed
RA
choosing as ruler
his son HORUS (Horushawk   seated god)
or
some say
the day we set up
the holiday
of meeting: the corpse which is OSIRIS

                             and
                      his father
during the making
of battle
by the gods
when the commander giving orders
was OSIRIS   Lord Amentet

What is it then?
Amentet (the world   under earth   out West)

the making of the souls
              (bowl of burning incense   bearded Horushawk)
of the gods
when the commander commanding was OSIRIS
in Set-Amentet
    (mountain/desert land and   the world   under earth   out West)
Set-Amentet   others call
Amentet
is
that which is
which makes
RA
stand and fight for it
when a god
any god
comes into it

I know the god
that god is in it.

Who is he then?

OSIRIS he is
others call RA
his name
the cock   (horizontal cock raining seedwater)
is RA's
when he fucks in strength
with
himself

I am
bennubird /the phoenix/
that bennubird which is
in Heliopolis /SunTown/

I am the doer executing
the book
of those madelings   alive now
and later

Who is he then?

He is OSIRIS
others say:
his own corpse is he
other people say
his shitting and pissing
!!!
those creations alive
now and later
make his corpse
others say
!!!

Eternity   (rooster   looping ropewick   SunDisk)
he is and
he lasts forever

Eternity is the day
!!!
He-lasts-forever is
Night
!!!
I am AMSU   (Standard)
in his seeming   (coming out)
his feathers on my head

Who is this then?
AMSU is HORUS
father's avenger
born coming out of godhouse

FRAGMENTS FROM MOUSAIOS

From Mousaios, the reputed son and secretary of Orpheus, a Greek text traditionally dated c. 1000 B.C., drawn from contemporaneous Phoenician and Egyptian sources. Text: Diels-Kranz, *Die Fragmente der Vorsokratiker,* Vol. 1. Numbers according to Diels-Kranz.

3. the eagle lays three eggs, two he hatches, one he leaves

5. but the fields give life to the leaves
    some die on the ash trees
    others live on

    our life those leaves

8.   The Story of Zeus Goat Skin Wearer

            When Zeus was born
            Rhea gave him to Themis
            Themis gave him to Amalthea
            but she gave him to Goat
            Goat, daughter of the Sun
            raised him in a cave on Crete
            where his father, Kronos
            couldn't find him

            she fed him her milk

            he grew up
            he fought the Titans

            since he didn't have any weapons
            the oracle told him
            "use Goat's skin for your shield
            it can't be hurt, besides
            Gorgon's head is in the middle"
            that's what he did
            and the skin stretched twice as large

Goat's bones he wrapped in another skin
gave them life, then life beyond death
set her up there among the stars

that's why we call Zeus "Goat Skin Wearer"

11. She-earth spoke an understanding word
Fiery, famous Earth-Shaker's helper, agreed

14. Pit was first and Night
the first goddess

16. Comets fall up from Ocean
into Sky where they are born

THE ORPHIC COSMOGONY
ACCORDING TO EUDEMOS

The "usual" Orphic cosmology according to Eudemos. A Greek text from the fourth century B.C. from Greek sources, c. 700–600 B.C. Text: a combination of two fragments, one from Damascius, *De Principiis,* the other from a critic of the second or third century A.D., Achilles Statius of Byzantium, both in Diels-Kranz, *Die Fragmente der Vorsokratiker,* Vol. 1.

Chronos

then FireAir   Gap
                         for everything that is
          Egg
                 (this is the first three)

the second three

          brooding
          Egg is seeded as 1. God
                              2. WhiteBright Robe
                              3. Cloud

     from the second three Phanes

               the third three
                    1. Metis who is mind
                    2. Erikepaios who is power
                    3. Phanes who is father

but what happened to Egg?

               shell is sky
                    membrane FireAir

THE ORPHIC COSMOGONY
ACCORDING TO ATHENAGORAS

A Greek text from the fourth century A.D. from older Greco-Roman Orphic sources, probably dating back to the time of *Sacred Stories* (sixth century B.C.). Text: Kern, *Orphicorum Fragmenta*.

Water

      from him Mud

               they had a child
                   the dragon snaked
                       lion-headed
                  god-faced between
             Chronos/Heracles

      Heracles laid a giant egg

           so filled by father Chronos

                it split

        the top sky Ouranos
        the bottom earth Gea

             and a god double-bodied . . . [Phanes?]

Ouranos slept with Gea
      girls:
        Klotho
        Lachesis
        Atropos
      boys:
        The Hundred-handed: Kottos Gyges Briareus
        The Cyclops: Brontes Steropes Arges

FROM PHERECYDES OF SYROS,
THE SEVEN NOOKS

Fragments from *The Seven Nooks* of Pherecydes of Syros.
A Greek text from the early seventh century B.C. Text: Diels-
Kranz, *Die Fragmente der Vorsokratiker,* Vol. 1, except for
1a. which is in Damascius, *De Principiis* (Ruelle, ed.). Numbers heading sections correspond to the numbered fragments
in Diels-Kranz.

1.

Z—Day   Time   She-earth
the always living

She-earth became our earth
Z—Day gave her earth for her honorable share

1a.

Chronos took his come
and slapped together
            wind   fire   water
            who split into 5 nooks
            wombs of the other gods

                    FiveNook

            making   FiveWorld[s]

2.

            The Story of the Flying Tree of Earth
            (on which She hung the web of cloth)

they are building houses for Z—Day
many houses huge houses
they put everything he'll need into them
they give men and women to serve him
and anything else he might need

when everything is ready
they have the wedding

on the third day of the wedding
Z—Day makes a web of cloth
a large and lovely mantle
he embroiders Earth and Ocean on it
and the houses of Ocean

[he gives it to his bride She-earth
he says to her]
"because you wish to marry
I give you this for honorable share
take pleasure in me
join me in love"

people say
this was the first rite of the unveiling
this is how the custom arose
among gods and men

after she receives the web of cloth
she says to him

3.

when he was about to make the world
Z—Day changed into Eros

he made the world out of contradictions
he drove agreement and love through it
he extended it into one throughout

4.

Kronos and Snake went to war
they raised up armies
they challenged each other and fought
then they made an agreement
whoever fell into Ocean first lost
the winner to be Sky-master

this is the beginning
of the mysteries of the Titans and Geagants
who people say fought the gods

and the stories   the Egyptians tell
of ⎧TYPHOON and Horus and Osiris
  ⎩Seth

5.

below our part of the world
is the share of Tartaros the Terrible

Snatchers and Hurricane
Northwind's daughters
stand guard there

whoever injures him
Zeus throws Tartaros

6.

hollows, ditches, caves, gates
riddles through which
souls pass and repass
this men call birth and death

the ordered world is a cave

7.

seed pours out

12.

the gods call a table *thyoros*
because that's where people
put out food for them

13.

Zeus and Hera are not the parents of the gods

13a.

gods eat immortality

FROM THE *SACRED STORIES*
OF ONOMACRITOS (?)

This Greek text was also known as the *Rhapsodic Theogony*, possibly compiled by Onomacritos, an early editor of Homer, c. 550 B.C. It was taken from Greco-Phoenician sources after 1100 B.C. and formed the Orphics' major sacred book. A full listing of the fragments is found at the end of this selection. "[. . .]" denotes material added for narrative continuity. ". . ." denotes material omitted. "***" denotes gaps in the original Greek text. " '. . .' " denotes verses cited by the ancients as stemming directly from Orpheus himself c. 1000 B.C. "⟨. . .⟩" denotes words which may be disregarded.

1.

[I, Orpheus, said]

' King Apollo
     Leto's son
    shooting from afar
         Phoibos of power '

        Lord   day son who hits everything
               with the arrows of your ray

          even though   far away
       unsullied can do-er ' see-all
   lording dier and deathless alike '

           who sees everyone
         king of gods and men

' Sun rising on golden wing '
     Helios in air on precious wing

                ' I heard the 12th voice come from you '
                I listened to the god voice
                in twelves
                [or: twelve times]

     ' when you came in brightness   shooter from afar
              divine testifier '
          when you spoke to me
       I witnessed you shining in the farness
              [tell me
                  how   it all began]

2.
[& Apollo told me:]
START
          ⟨workman in⟩ Chronos/'Olam
                  makes FireAir
              that Chaos/Egg a belt rings
                  yes dark cloud
                gripping in her domes
            everything under FireAir
                  but   before   above   inside
    PHANES   who made them
      whom you can't touch   can't hold
         fathermother of Night   FireAir
             and all the diacosm
    [slept] in gloom in Chaos/Egg
       wrapped in FireAir
                Earth   unseen shadowy
    Light/Phanes
             shattering FireAir
             piercing Chaos
         blinding Earth and everything else
  Phanes—Metis—Erikepaios [the three in one] who mean
         'Light Giver of Life'
          from himher
            bodiless beginnings

                              & sun   moon   means   stars
                   earth   sea   the world   seen and unseen

3.

[They tell it another way]

          Chronos/'Olam ▽ Rhea [Lady Hyle]
                         Egg

                                   remember?

Egg   in Chronos   in time
             spinning   warming
                    makes SkyHeaven
                           who is round   half
                                   & screwed   on top of Earth

Egg filled to bursting
                one chrome
                      one skin   & color
                            his body: phantasy
                   think of a peacock's egg
                                   inside
                                   the 1,000 colors of its fan
                             so Egg grew
                                   stocked with the Wind
                                        that blows out
                                        the endless colors
                                                of everything
                                                that breathes

Egg   like a top
             turning in the currents of Lady Hyle
                    see there every change light brings

                inside:
                    the godwind racing up and down
                        the malefemale
                            doing it by thought
                    Phanes [Metis Erikepaios]
                            bright Phancy
                    the torch
                            firing the diacosm
                    'telesphoros'
                            [beginning   ending
                            year accomplisher
                            to fulfill purpose
                            ordering managing favoring]
                                lightning bug
                                lamp in the water

yes   warm   hot   ripe   Egg
            broke on the inside
                        ' when the [clay?] gaping egg
                                yawns: cracks: '
                            Phanes
                                steps out
                                    to make the world
                                        a harmony
                                        that coheres

    4.

    for Phanes

                        authors all the gods
                            built them a sky
                                & for their children
                    ' for those who do not die
                        he made a home that does not wear out '

    31.

                        seeded the Golden Race [in Metis]

5.

        and was the   first king of the gods

6.

he/she has a number: 12

        from the completed number of the 3rd
        & of the 4th that brings to birth—
            worker in 'mixing and mingling'
            cupping the bright diacosm of the gods

$$3 \quad \times \quad 4 \quad = 12$$

starts
1
&
2
of
3
&
4

1 = FireAir   (+ 1)
2 = Gap/Chaos(+ 1)
3 = Egg   who is completed (by +1)
4 = *Phanes*
        # ' seen to 4 eyes everythere '

      Erikepaios

5.

    Metis

      ' fearful angel '
      carrying glorious godsperm
      whom the Blessed on Olympos
      call
         ' Phanes FirstBorn '

3.

    then Phanes goes away
          sits in one of the crags of skyheaven
             [in the cave of Daughter Night]
          where in secret ways
                he lights up
           [the comings and goings   of]
          boundless time

9.

      don't ask questions
        give up

          Phanes and Night rule skyheaven

31.

           she the second queen
           holding the scepter
              he/she made

9.

. . .

seated in the nook of her cave
          they last out time
              in the inmost unseen cryptic adytos
             Phanes
               and Daughter Night
           who gives the gods
            oracles
           [that never fail]

    call them
     and you wouldn't be wrong
        malefemale
      fathermother
          sunmoon   set among the Wanderers
          theone   that equals everyone

[* * *]

     the krater
        mixing bowl
          where cupped
          in their embrace
          everysoul   sees life

8.

     Iynges
       [wrynecks
         birds of magic

       four spoked wheels

        (the malefemale)
      Pothos (Hipeḥ) Eros]

7.

[Adrasteia serves them]
    alone the goddess of those who remain in Night
            Melissos' and Amaltheia's daughter
    from their unswerving forethought
        ' pretty girl Ida and sperm sister Adrasteia '
          who takes   who holds within her
      the measure of all practice in the diacosm
        inside and out

               outside their Cave
she whacks the   ' big bronze kettledrums Night gave her '
           by the door
          pounding drum tambourine cymbal
           so all can hear her laws

11.

‘ [beneath the stars that] see white

[that] glitterflash in the dusky cloth of Night ’

8.

‘ Phanes broke the virgin flower
of Daughter [Night] ’

10.

children:
Skyheaven/Uranos
Earth/Ge
The Cyclops
The Hundred Handed
Skyheaven was their first child
he shone
because his father was god of light

8.

he fucked his sister [Ge]
just like Daddy did [Night] Daughter

12.

the children

31.

whom Ge hid from their father the 3rd king Skyheaven

12.

    seven girls lovely and pure
    who roll their eyes in come hithers

        Themis
        wise Tethys
        Mnemosyné whose hair hangs down
        happy Theia
        Dioné—especially pretty
        Phoibé
        Rhea mother of king Zeus

    seven boys   wooly haired kings

        Koios
        big Krios
        strong Phorkys
        Kronos
        Ocean
        Hyperion
        Iapetos

14. [This is what Ocean and Kronos did]

Ocean   flows   backward   he hurries on himself
    it is better to say:
        he returns
          leading himself in circles
         around his mother Earth
           whom he holds inside himself
      ' the circle of lovely untiring rippling Ocean:
          rows around Earth
       keeping her all inside his swirls '

31. & 16.

    [But Kronos rebelled]
        caught his dad
          cut off his balls
        became the 4th king
         maker of the Silver Race

FROM THE "SACRED STORIES" OF ONOMACRITOS (?)   107

28.

           he was   'first to think around corners'
           made everything return
                to itself

13.

                  Mixer Kronos
          hair on his chin always black
             meaning that people then
                refused   old age
                and were always young

15.

[Kronos fucked his sister Rhea

              children:
                the Olympians
                especially Zeus

      Kronos swallowed them all: except Zeus
      Rhea gave him a stone instead
         sent Zeus to Crete
         to Dicté's Cave
         where Amaltheia Nursed him
         & the Kouretes
            beating their
                shields
         distracted daddy

  when he grew up
        he got his revenge

                just like his father before him]

16.

        caught him with honey
                filled up Kronos with beer
                          drunk
                   he passed out
Night had told him

        ' if you see your father under tall oaks
          drunk with deeds of raspy buzzing bees
          tie '   him   ' up '

               tied him up   cut off his balls
                   ' cutting and being cut '
               o
               fathers and sons

17.

     the balls hit water and floated
         all around
              white foam spun
     in Hours' circles
           Eniautos built inside (this spermy egg)
           the modest Lady of Generation:

      [Aphrodite]
     who in her palms
       as she was being born
       took the first of jealousy and deceit

31.

18.

5th King Zeus
     before making anything
         went to the oracles of Night
          who filled him with thought
          beginning things

and released his doubt:

        'father be the mother'

Zeus said:

     ' Eternal Night
           highest god   *maia*/nurse
                             how
                  tell me
                       how am **I**
                  strong heart
        to make
           the beginnings
              of gods?

19.

        how shall I be and have one and all
              and each thing separately? '

[Oracle Night:]

     ' swallow everything that nameless FireAir [Phanes is]
        in his/her body
           skyheaven
           immense earth
           sea
           & all stars that make the pictures
           skyheaven locks in circles

20.

        stretch a chain
           golden links of FireAir
     to bind [the diacosm Phanes the 1st World] '

21.

[so] Phanes First Born
          loveliest of those minded
                     powered
                       & alive of self
          loneliest justicier of hisher making

Zeus swallowed
          on advice of Night

      ' Phanes Erikepaios held
                  the body of everything
          in his hollow belly
             mixed in hisher bones & flesh
                the godpower
so that with himher [inside] everything could be made
      of Zeus
      once anew '

22.

      ' so with himher [inside]
          [The 2nd World] was made of Zeus once anew
             height of skyheaven and fireair
             couch of barren sea
                & glorious earth
        huge Ocean   Earth's deepest Tartara
           rivers
        sea more than enough
      and everything else
          including:
      all the gods and goddesses
          deathless and happy

whatever was will be one is born
mixing and mingling in Zeus's belly '

20.

        and he laid down a golden chain
                                 [binding sky and earth]
              as Night told him

24.

But Phanes will return

31.

      he is Dionysos the 6th king

              [Zeus lives in a palace on Olympos
                      married to Sister Hera
                fucks Semelé
                        Cadmos' daughter

                                their child
                                    Dionysos
        whom he hides on Crete from Hera's anger]

23.

        where the Kouretes put on their armor
                and danced for him
         [as they did to save his father]

25.

[but Hera found out
        she sent the Titans,   Ge's boys, to kill him]
             they snuck up   amused him with toys
              then   tore him to bits
                ate the result daintily

23.

      these are the toys they used:
      ' pine cone, rhomb, puppets

> silver apples from the daughters of Hesperos
> who speak with clear voice   '
> plus a die, sphere, top, mirror,
> and fleece

27.

[say this about the Titans]

the Purification from frankincense

Titans

> shining children
> of Skyheaven & Earth
> fathers before
> of our fathers

Titans

> beneath Earth
> in the wombs of Tartaros
>
> tending the wells
> that feed dying men
> whom pain never frees

Titans

> of saltsea
> of wingbirdair
> of earthhome
>
> please
> keep your anger away
> if one of you comes to my house

25.

        Zeus found out what they did
           he smashed them with a thunderbolt

        from the soot of the smoke of their bombing
           he made the stuff we're remade of:

28.

                the Titanic Race: us
              part cannibal
              part light

     whom Zeus taught
       worse things than Phanes and Kronos
       taught their folk :

                ' plan ahead
                    get it right '
Golden Silver Titanic: these are all the kinds there are

25.

         part Titan
           part Dionysos
              so   don't kill yourself
          —you can't anyway—
          the body is not a prison
            despite what they say:
               soma/sema

29.

     [life and death: no difference
       you can always make a comeback
       remember:]

       ' birds & beasts &
            the guilt-ridden tribes of men '
hermeneutic: beasts and birds/ the consumed nations of man

' the burdens of earth
                    hammered out bodies
                                nothing through nothing '
hermeneutic: the onus of earth/ made-up bodies
                          nothing is born   nothing dies

26.

Zeus couldn't get over his boy's death
                    made a plaster statue of him in Crete
      put in it the heart Sister Athené had saved from the Titans
          right where   he'd framed the lineaments of the chest

                    for tomb built him a temple
                                his pedagogue Silenus the priest

Cretans
          to soften his pain and theirs
                          keep his deathday holy
                every third year   sacred
          doing again in order everything Dionysos did
                          and suffered when he died
                they chew up a living bull
          they race through the woods
                          crying out his name
                                real
                          there is no pretense
                endless chanting dancing ecstasy
flutes scream
                          cymbals smash
      a top whirling on a string
                          recalls the bull's hoarse bellow

                bacchants carry the box Athené put his heart in
                      and the toys that beguiled him

this is how a god who couldn't be buried was made

30.

[sing this song for] Zeus

                                   : first
                                   : last

                                   : lashing lightning thunder thunder flash

           Zeus : head
                : body of

everything that is :

                                   : cock
                                   : cunt

                                   : stand of the bowl of earth
                                            of sky of stars

                                   : King
           Zeus : who does it all

            one : dyne
                : demon

                                   : kingbody of everything wheeling into one

                                   : night   day

           Zeus : Metis   first and subtlest (mist of) air

           Zeus : Eros   who is every delight
                                        don't fight his powerflesh

           face : lightpricked sky

         beard : gold   glare   stars   hung   in air
                              two   gold bull's horns
                                        flashing right and left

                                   : sunrise   & set
                                   : walkway of the gods of sky

          eyes : sun   and   measuring/answering moon

         mind : that does not deceive
                   royal FireAir that does not wear out

```
  everything : listens
             : bows to him

          he : notes   purposes   points

         ear : that hears
               your voice cry shout doomscream

        Zeus : deathless head
             : untiring thought

        body : muscles of light no end
               at peace dauntless strong boned

shoulders  chest  back : air hissing everywhere
                              his wings span out
                           so that he is absent nowhere

     stomach : earthmotherall   mountain crests
               puckered ocean sea ruffling

waist and belt :

        feet : fixed deep in roots
               in moldy pit
               Earth's buried anchor


        Zeus : who swallows all
             : to once anew bring out in cheerful

dayfather[mother] :

             : planting again enroots his godbody
```

An alternate conclusion for *Sacred Stories* taken from the *Clementine Homilies*. This follows the withdrawal of Phanes into Night's cave.

Lady Hyle
    now a hollow nook
        lay down under Chronos/'Olam
            submitting to time
      he filled her up again
she "turned"   curdled
      boiling with children
    1. Pluto   king of the dead
           who is heavy   sank down   beneath Earth
           whom Chronos/'Olam swallowed
                all of him
              rough and dirty
       for that is his return   his recession
    2. Poseidon   who is water
           whatever floats to the surface of Lady Hyle
    3. Zeus   clear fire
          whom Chronos/'Olam could not swallow
            for he climbed into Skyheaven
             rolling up like a ball doing somersaults
        burning off the wet
            drinking it and breathing out
            made Metis   subtlest [mist of] wind
from/on a crest of FireAir   which he bit off and swallowed
           he shaped Pallas
               the Ball Player
               Balloter
               Palper
    whose mindedness he needed to make the world
from jabbing Zeus   from burning Fire
     Air reached the place   they call Hera
Sister   because Air   is so clear
Wife   because as in woman   Fire can only come   in Air

BIBLIOGRAPHY FOR *SACRED STORIES*

Numbers on left-hand side of text correspond to those assigned the fragments below. All fragments found in: Kern, *Orphicorum Fragmenta* (*OF*).

1. Malalas, *Chronography, OF* #62
2. Ibid., *OF* #65
3. 'Apion' as quoted in the *Clementine Homilies, OF* #56
4. Lactantius, *Divine Institutes, OF* #89
5. Quoted in Proclos, *On Plato's Timaios, OF* #85
6. Hermias, *On Plato's Phaedrus, OF* #76
7. Ibid., *OF* #105
8. Summarized from *OF* #98
9. Proclos, *On Plato's Timaios, OF* #104
10. Condensed from *OF* #109
11. *Orphic Hymn VII, OF* #100
12. Quoted in Proclos, *On Plato's Timaios, OF* #114
13. Proclos, *On Hesiod's Works and Days, OF* #130
14. Eustathius, *Guide to Dionysos, OF* #115
15. Summarized from Hesiod's *Theogony*
16. Porphyry, *The Cave of the Nymphs, OF* #154. Also see Proclos, *On Plato's Cratylos, OF* #137
17. Quoted in Proclos, *On Plato's Cratylos, OF* #127
18. Proclos, *On Plato's Timaios, OF* #164
19. Ibid., *OF* #165
20. Ibid., *OF* #166
21. Ibid., *OF* #167
22. Ibid., *OF* #167
23. Clement of Alexandria, *Protreptica* (*Exhortations*), *OF* #34
24. Proclos, *On Plato's Timaios, OF* #85
25. Olympiodoros, *On Plato's Phaedo, OF* #220
26. Firmicus Maternus, *The Errors of Profane Religion, OF* #214
27. *Orphic Hymn 38, OF* #220
28. Proclos, *On Plato's Republic, OF* #140
29. Malalas, *Chronography, OF* #76
30. Quoted by Porphyry in Eusebius, *Preparation for the Gospel, OF* #168
31. Proclos, *On Plato's Timaios, OF* #107

FROM APOLLONIUS OF RHODES,

THE ARGONAUTICA

A Greek text of the third century B.C. from the *Argonautica* of Apollonius of Rhodes. Text: Diels-Kranz, *Die Fragmente der Vorsokratiker*, Vol. 1.

Orpheus picked up his lyre

" Earth & Sea & Sky

who once were One

Hate split up

these are the eternal reminders

stars
moon
sun paths

then the mountains rose

the rivers sang
to the nymphs in their streams
who answered their song

was born the creeping the crawling
whoever goes on all fours

Ophion Snake &
Eurynomé wide ruler
on snow topped Olympos

he like Kronos in his hand's force
she like Rhea

but they fell into Ocean's waves

then Kronos and Rhea
        were lords of the Titans

    Zeus still young

      still child thinking in Dicté's cave

not yet made strong by thunder lightning
          and lightning flash

       which the Cyclops gave him
         to give him glory "

FROM THE *ORPHIC ARGONAUTICA*

A Greek text, c. second century A.D. Text: *Orphic Argonautica* 11.419–32, in Kern, *Orphicorum Fragmenta* #29.

I picked up my lyre
song came
flooding my mouth
    first the black song of old Chaos
        who barters birth
      then Sky coming to limit
      Earth with her wide teats
        sea sounding the deeps
    oldest self-beginning ending wily Love

      everything was born
        everything pulled apart
     from one another

    Kronos the Destroyer

        Zeus who loves thunder

     kings of the gods who never do without

I sang of the birth of the younger armed gods

   who argued (with the Titans)

      the Titans who rent Brimos Bacchos:

      the populous birth of feeble men

throughout the narrow cave
the song of my lyre
coursing through the honeyed voice

Elemental Creation

II. FALLING

FROM ARISTOPHANES, *THE BIRDS*

A Greek text by Aristophanes, c. fifth century B.C.; the cosmogony here dates back to c. 1000 B.C. Text: Aristophanes, *The Birds*, in Kern, *Orphicorum Fragmenta* #1.

first   Gap   Night   deep Dark   abyss Tartaros

                            no air earth or sky

then in deep Dark's bottomless wombs
Night on black wings laid the wind egg

as the seasons went round
              there hatched Love the Desired
      who shoots light forth
        from the gold wings on his back
        who has the body of wind turned on tornado spins

at night he blended in Gap down below in abyss Tartaros
          laying/hatching the eggs of our race
                he first led us to light

before Love mixed in
          there were no deathless gods
once he had let everything go
           into everything else
    sea sky air
        as well as the gods' imperishable race
                    were born

A Latin text by Hyginus, c. first century B.C./A.D., taken from traditional Near Eastern sources dating back to c. 1400 B.C. Text: Hyginus, *Fabulae* (Rose, ed.).

a giant egg fell into the Euphrates

fish pushed it to shore

where doves sat down and warmed it

it hatched

out came Venus

later called the Syrian Goddess

(Ashtaroth)

THREE MIDRASHIM

FROM THE *PIRKE DE RABBI ELIEZER*

From the Hebrew text *Pirke de Rabbi Eliezer*, c. A.D. 150.
Text: *Pirke de Rabbi Eliezer*, ed. Zisberg and Halter.

. . . .

created 8 things the first day

sky	light	tohu	wind
earth	dark	bohu	water

"& the *wind* of Elohim moved on the *water*"

(1)

THE ORIGIN OF SKY

was from light of his own robe
he took & stretched it
like a robe the skies
were rolling out from
he figured that should do it
in Shadai's words   "shall do"
—became his name then—
then firmed it up (they say)
"thy covering of thyself
"with light
"is like a robe
"the way thou stretchest the sky out
" 's like a curtain"

(2)

THE ORIGIN OF EARTH

took snow or ice
—'twas underneath his throne—
& dropped it on
the waters
then they became congealed
earth's crust was formed from it
(they say)
"he tells the snow
"be earth"

(3)

COSMOLOGIES

sky's curtain hooks 're set in
ocean's water
's set between the ends of
sky & earth
the ends of sky 're spread across
his ocean's waters
"are his house posts set into
"his waters"

. . . .

that we should see the sky from inside
—& call it dome—
was like a basket
maybe like a tent
stretched out & with the tent flaps
downward
the dome stretched high & far
the people crowd in
feet set on the earth
& everyone inside the tent
the way the sky's ends

touch the earth
dome stretches upward
& all life's lived
inside it
like a tent (they say)
"he spreads them like a tent
"to dwell in"

. . . .

4 winds or quarters
made for earth
1 east
1 south
1 west
1 north
from the quarter facing east
light seeks the world
from the quarter facing south
sweet dew   sweet rain
from the quarter facing west
the treasuries of snow & hail
bring cold & heat into the world
& hard rain
from the quarter facing north
darkness moves out
"fourth quarter's incomplete (he says)
"made but unfinished
"anyone who says he's god
"can come & work on it
"complete it
"then everyone will say
"this one's a god"

FROM THE FIFTH ELEGY OF MAXIMIAN

From the Fifth Elegy of Maximian of Etruria who lived c.
A.D. 600 and holds the distinction of being the last pagan Latin
poet. Text: in Bährens, ed., *Poetae Latini Minores,* Vol. 5.

cock holidays busy plowing
cock   wealth   joy   giver
I weep for you
            lost in a whirl of tears
although no song I have
is worth you

when I burned
tidal fire bursting my soul
you soothed
giving me a game to play

guard who never slept
but made do with me
            whether I laughed or cried

with my secrets
and their secret resting place
I trusted you
standing straight and true
in internal service
all night long

who did it?
made you lose the feeling power?
when will you lift your coxcomb
to stab me again?

now soft and bloodless
you bow to death

I am helpless to touch you into life
sing you into me

you look ready for the grave

rightly said :
"what no longer does dies"
. . .

his failing
not my loss
but everyone's
chaos come back again

cock made people cattle bird and beast
on this globe whatever breathes

take him away
male and female die
man's mind not join woman's
in union that makes their bodies one

take him away
lovely woman loses her price
the men go for nothing

there's no sun-bit gold
                in a crystalled gem

dead cock cheats
like a farm sown with salt
working towards death

but cock live
then we trust ourselves
we keep our secrets safe and holy

come cock
joy today
a future tomorrow

the universe is yours
the Kings above   below
chose to give you their rods
surrendering to joy
they do not lie
                groveling at your feet

. . .

ever since the gods
drove the giants from the sky
cock you throw the triple-sheeted lightning bolt
for angered Zeus

teaching the tigress love
and the lion kindness

even Wisdom, this world's Queen
gives you her hand
obeying your commands

equally strong and patient
you amaze
those you've beaten
you love yet
you enjoy losing
lying down in defeat
once more to rise loving
again to lose to win

Elemental Creation

III. DIVIDING

Autonomic and Aliyan Texts

A. AUTONOMIC TEXTS

DAMASCIUS,
THE EGYPTIAN COSMOLOGY

The Egyptian Cosmology according to Damascius; a Greek text, c. A.D. 500, from an Egyptian source, c. 500 B.C. Text: Damascius, *De Principiis* (Ruelle, ed.).

one

one who is called by the name of unknown shadows

(say three times)

two

Water and Sand
or Sand and Water

their child

KA-ME[M?]PHIS I
[Ptah?]

father of

KA-ME[M?]PHIS II
[Isis?]

father of

KA-ME[M?]PHIS III
[Horus?]

they are the world   the diacosm

AN INCANTATION AGAINST TOOTHACHE

An Akkadian cosmogony attached to an incantation in order to assure control, c. 800 B.C. Text: *Cuneiform Texts from Babylonian Tablets, etc., in the British Museum.*

Start:

Sky made sky
sky made dirt
dirt made flow-ers
flow-ers made canals
canals made swamp

swamp made worm

From *De Principiis* by Damascius, a Greek text, c. A.D. 500, from a Babylonian source, c. 1000 B.C. Text: *De Principiis* (Ruelle, ed.).

there are two
{ TAUTHÉ   { APASON
{ (Tiamat)   and   { (Apsu)

{ TAUTHÉ
{ (Tiamat)   mother of the gods
{ APASON
{ (Apsu)   her lover

their child { MOYMIS—who is everything we see
{ (Mummu)

and then they had
{ DACHÉ   and   { DACHOS
{ (Laḫmu)   and   { (Laḫamu)

and then
{ KISSARÉ   and   { ASSOROS
{ (Kišar)   { (Anšar)

and they had three children
{ ANOS
{ (Anu)

{ ILLINOS
{ (Enlil)

{ AOS
{ (Ea)

{ AOS' and { DAUKÉ'S   son: { BELOS   the Maker
{ (Ea)   { (Damkinna)   { (BEL)
{ (Marduk)

SANCHUNIATHON,

THE *PHOENICIAN HISTORY*

A Greek translation, c. second century A.D., translated into
Greek by Philo of Byblos from the works of the Phoenician
poet, Sanchuniathon, who lived, possibly in Byblos as well,
c. 1300–900 B.C. The present fragmentary text is found in:
Eusebius, *Praeparatio Evangelica,* in *Patrologia Graeca,* Migne
(ed.).

Prefaces by various hands

Eusebius, *Preparation for the Gospel* (Fourth century A.D.)

The gods, according to the ancients, are representations of our
moral nature and, in the words of the oracle, the invention of images
for them marked the beginning of their disappearance. But this is not
true: in point of fact the gods, having sprung or rather initiating from
the Phoenicians and the Egyptians, passed from them to other nations
—in particular to the Greeks. That this is true is confirmed by the
history it is now time for us to review: the Phoenician "testament."

Porphyry, *Against the Christians* (Third century A.D.)

The truest history of the Semitic peoples is contained in that
Sanchuniathon of Beirut because his most closely agrees with the
topology and onomastics of the region. Furthermore he used as raw
material the records of Hierobalus, the priest of Ieuo [pronounced
"Yeh-woh"], and dedicated his book to Adibalos, the king of Beirut,
since it had been approved by the king and his scholars. These men
lived before the Trojan War, almost about the time Moses did, as the
Phoenician king-lists show. Sanchuniathon, who fell in love with his
subject, collected and wrote his work from the records of the local
cities in Phoenicia and from the priestly registers. It is further said he
lived during the reign of Semiramis, the Assyrian queen whom the

chroniclers tell us flourished either before the time of the Trojan War or else was its contemporary. And this is the History that Philo of Byblos translated into Greek.

Philo of Byblos: *Translator's Preface* (Second century A.D.)

Sanchuniathon, a man of great learning and desirous of still more knowledge, interested himself in the early history of all peoples, beginning from the creation of the world. Painstakingly he researched the history of Taautos since he knew full well that of all men born under the sun Taautos was the only inventor of letters and record keeping. With him, as most appropriate, he began his *History:* with him whom the Egyptians call Thoyth, the Alexandrians Thoth, and the Greeks Hermes.

But the most recent of hierologues who reject the real even before they begin to write, treating of one thing in the guise of another, have striven to invent a fabulous mythology. They do not stop at this, but even shape imaginary analogues between this world and the conditions of the cosmos, establishing mysteries and wrapping everything in a cloud of darkness and ignorance so that one cannot easily find out the truth of what in fact did take place. But Sanchuniathon, who happened upon the writings of the Ammoneans, composed secretly in their temples (and naturally not known to all men), set to work to master them. Having done that, he was able to write and, most importantly, to put away the received myths and their attendant allegories. However, the priests who came later, wishing to restore the mythic character, swathed his *History* in silence and obscurity, whereupon the mystic sense arose, even among the Greeks, it not having touched them previously.

For the sake of explaining the *History* itself and its contents, it is necessary to make clear right from the start that the ancient barbarians, principally the Phoenicians and the Egyptians (from whom the rest of the world received their traditions), worshipped as gods whatever contributed to the health and well-being of communal life. In particular it was the Phoenicians' habit to affix their kings and whoever among them divinely conspicuous to the elements of the cosmos, but they knew no other gods than those of the natural world, sun, moon, and the other wandering stars (all that has grown out of connection with them), so that some of their gods are mortal and others are not.

I. *Creation*

All father Ruaḥ Air, dark blowing clouding

a wind a cloud : and Gap Koḥot'erev chaos black as Erebos

swirling in gloom throughout that first long age,

boundless endless

Ruaḥ falls in love with his parts

sprays himself with come

Hipeḥ, Desire

beginning things

though Ruaḥ did not know it yet,

the child of himself : Mot

whom some call mud

and others mold, from her

zera' the spores of creation the genetices of the world,

then there were others :

the ḥayot not possessed of sense,

from them the Tzofe-šemin who were,

and Mot the Egg burst into light

and the sun and the moon and the stars and the big ones

w h e n s h e h a d b u r s t i n t o l i g h t
      ' s splendor
her strong
        heat
struck
     land
      and
        sea
       '
           clouded
    blew
rained
    they stood apart
    each moved from their place
    from the blow of her heat
    and flew up back into Ruaḥ
  meeting rubbing
         crushing together
            thunder lightning flash

  at that noise
  the Tzofe-šemin awake
and were frightened
and began to move out on the land and sea male and female

II. *The Nomoi*

from the Wind that blows from the Gulf
from Qol-pias and Baau his wife
the first diers
Ḥava and Adam Qadmun
Aion and Protogonos
Ḥava found out
how to eat the fruit of trees

from them
in Phoenicia
their children Qen and Qenat
Birth and Tribe
who in drought
stretch forth their hands
to the sun
master of the sky:
calling him Ba'al-šamin
Day Father

from them N'er, 'Eš, Lahav
Light, Fire, Flame:
from the rubbing of sticks
and teaching the use of it

from them
Nefilim the Titans
and the mountains they name
correspond in size:
Qasiun, Lebanun, Hermun, Tabor

from them
Šame-merom/Hypsuranios and 'Esav/Beš
named for their mothers:
as women then
fucked without shame
any they met

Šame-merom
lived in Tyre
building huts
of reed and papyrus strands

he quarreled with 'Esav
his brother: who wore
the clothes of the beasts
he caught and skinned

Then it rained in Tyre:
the wind drove the trees
against each other
and made them burn
and so the place
was stripped of wood

Though 'Esav
catching a tree
lopped the branches off
and paddled out to sea:
the first

And dedicating two pillars
to Wind and Fire:
poured the blood of the beasts
he caught over them

from their children:
Šet and Sidon
man of the wilds
man of the seas:
the hunting and fishing clans

from them
the Iron Worker
Kothar:
singer enchanter speaker diviner
Hephaistos:
fashioner of the hook, bait, line, and raft
who were worshipped
once they died:

god of the trades and clans/ Malak the Worker
and his brother
built walls of brick

from Worker's people
Qen the Technites
and Autochthon
Adam Landsman

they chopped straw
mixed clay
cut it into bricks
dried in the sun
result: roofs

from them Šet and Sadé
Tiller and Stalker:
Stalker is
the great god of Byblos:
in Phoenicia they still carry
his statue
on an oxcart:
they built houses
with basements and courtyards
and rooms

from them 'Ilim and Nefilim
Farmers and Hunters
called Settlers and Nomads

their children
Amynos and Magos
Upright and Wise
built villages
and herded sheep

their children
Mish'or the Busy and Tzadoq the Just
discovered salt

from Mishor
Taaut
inventor of the alphabet:
whom the Egyptians call Thoyth
the Alexandrians Thoth
and the Greeks Hermes
three times master

from Tzadoq
the Dioskouroi or Cabeiroi or Corybantes or Samothraces:
the Kabirim who built the first ship
whose children
the first to pick herbs
cured snake bite
weaving charms from them

And in that time
lived 'Elion the "most high"
and his lady, Berut/Ba'alat
their home was Byblos

III. *The 3 Generations*

Adam Landsman
they called Uranos Shama
from the excellence
of his beauty
he names the upper world

Adamat Ge
his sister
naming the lower
the Earth

'Elion died
meeting beasts
and became a god:
his children poured out
and fed him
according to the rites

Adam
king in his place
married Adamat
and had by her:
'El
who is Kronos: and
Bet-'el: and
Dagon
who is Wheat Food God: and
Atlas Anatal(?)

Adam married
many times and had
many children by the concubines of heaven:

Adamat took that bitterly
and struck back with hard words
so they parted

Adam
came back
and filled her with children
by force and went away
whenever it was his mood
destroying them
when he could

many times
Adamat drove him back
gathering friends
about her
'El and Taaut
his secretary
protected her
and saved her honor

the children of 'El:
Persephoné 'Elat
that died virgin:
Athené 'Anat
who with Taaut

told him to forge
the iron sickle
and the iron spear

Taaut spoke
magic to the 'Elohim
the cronies of 'El:
wrought desire in them
to fight against Adam

and:
overthrew his father
seizing the kingship

they took
the lovely concubine
of Adam in that battle:
she carried his son
in her belly, but 'El
gave her in marriage
to Dagon, and in his house
she bore him Demarous
who is Ba'al Tamar

'El built a wall
around his house:
Byblos in Phoenicia,
the first city

He grew suspicious
of his brother Atlas
and threw him in a pit:
he listened to Taaut
and buried him

Then the children
of the Kabirim
ran their ships aground
at the foot of Mt. Qasiun
and built a temple there

'El killed his son Šadid
and cut off the head
of one of his daughters
with the iron sword:
he had no trust in them
he surprised all the gods
by his mindedness

Adam sent Astarté
and her two sisters
Amma Rhea and Dioné Ba'alt
to kill 'El
by their cunning:
but he fucked them
though his sisters
and married them

when Adam heard
he sent Heimarmené/Giddé
and Hora/No'ema to make war:
but 'El assimilated them
he kept them by his side

Then Adam created Bet'yl
the Baetylia
thinking to put life
into stones

to 'El:
seven daughters by Astarté,
Tanit the Titanides or Artemides:
seven sons by Rhea,
the youngest a god from birth:
and by Dioné girls:
and by Astarté the boys:
Pothos and Eros, Hipeḥ and Dūd

to 'El
by other women
in the Land beyond the River (Euphrates?):
three sons,

'El Again
Zeus/HaBa'al
and Reshef/Apollo

Dagon invented
the plow to furrow
the wheat field:
they called him
" a r o t r i o s "
"the plowman"

Tzadoq married one of the Tanit:
Asclepios/Ešmun
his child

At the same time
Yam and Tzefon
Pontos and Typhoon:
and Nereus/Nahar
HaBa'al's son
Yam's brother

And from Yam
Sidon her voice
so lovely in song
there came music forth

And from Yam
Tan/Poseidon
lord of the sea

Ba'al Tamar's son:
Mel-kart who is the (Tyrian) Herakles

then afterward:
Adam fought with Yam
Ba'al Tamar helped

Ba'al Tamar jumped into Yam
but Yam ran away

Ba'al Tamar said
"if I get away
I'll give you something to eat"

And in the 32nd year
of his kingship
inland
beside springs and brooks
'El caught his father
and tore out his balls
with his own hands:
Adam became god there
as breath left him
blood trickling down
drop by drop from the wound
into those springs and brooks,
today I could show you the spot

This is the story of Adam and all his people

The first and golden age of men: *meropes*

"who speak with clear articulate voice"

---

as the poets write

---

that blessed happiness of an ancient time

Astarté, the greatest
of goddesses, and Ba'al Tamar/Adonis
and Hadad
king of the gods
became lords of Phoenicia
'El approved

Astarté set a bull's head upon her own
as the sign of her power
circling the earth
she found a star fallen to earth
which she gave to Tyre
and consecrated on that holy isle

her name
the Phoenicians say
is also Aphrodite

'El in his journeyings
gave the queenship
of Attica to Anat

when the plague came
and death:
'El offered Adam
his only son burnt whole
he cut off the tip of his penis
forcing the 'Elohim
to do the same

when his son by Rhea
Mot died
he made him god:
to signify death to the Phoenicians
the Greeks call him
T h a n a t o s   P l u t o

'El gave his city Byblos
to the goddess Baaltis
whom the Greeks call Dioné
and Berytos to Tan
and the Kabirim: to both
the Farmers and the Sailors

of Yam
what they found:
they made god
in Berytos

Taaut before this
imitated the shapes
of Adam and the other gods:
of 'El and Dagon:
of all those who were with Adam
he struck the sacred stamp:
he gave to letters
their character

for 'El
he made the Seal of Kingship
four eyes that look
to the front and four behind
two of them closed in sleep
and two open on each side:
upon his shoulders
he set four wings
two spread in flight
two folded in rest
and the Seal reads,
'El sees and sleeps
sleeps and sees
flies at rest
rests in flight:
to each
of the other gods
he gave two wings
since they fly with 'El

to 'El
he gave two more wings
and put them on his head
one for the quality
of his mindedness
the other
for swiftness
of his thought

when 'El
came to the land
of the South Wind
he gave Taaut
for palace
the whole of Egypt

. . .

All this
the seven sons of Tzadoq
the Kabirim preserved

and their eighth brother
Ešmun as the god
Taaut told them to

IV. [*'Olam*] *the Dragon Snake*

Taaut made the dragon snake god
                     breath spirit and fire
             body so quick
                   you cannot see it
          though he has no hands or feet

spirals
    where he's going
         taking   leaving shape

                    never dies
                sheds his skin
                becoming young
                    renews his age

                ready to die
              he swallows himself

             you want to kill him?
          cut him first into pieces
              otherwise you never will

they call him { AGATHODAIMON the { MALAKH   Ba'al
           { PrettyDemon   { angel of

This text was originally discovered on a papyrus scrap in Egypt in 1957. It contains a commentary (in fragmentary form) by an unknown scholar c. third century B.C. on a now-lost cosmological poem by Alcman, a poet active in the eighth–seventh centuries B.C., who was born in Lydia in Asia Minor and worked mainly in Sparta. Text: in *Poetae Melici Graeci*, (Page, ed.). "[. . .]" denotes lost words supplied by papyrologists; ". . ." denotes lost letters; "x̱" denotes letter x has been restored; "x-y" denotes two possible readings, x or y; "/" denotes a full stop; "(. . .)" denotes translator's additions or explanatory words; "?" denotes a supposition; word or words in *italics* means it is being quoted by the ancient commentator from Alcman's lost original.

. . .

. ṇ . [
of all . . . [
someone-a *out of the p*[si
gn was born t[
mo[.] and then-from (sign?) ei . [(was born?)
way (a word which is derived) from way- . [. .] . [(making?)
for when unwrought timber stuff began to be shape[d
(by the skills of Thetis??)
a way as if (for) a start was born / indeed Alcman s[ays

___

the unwrought timberstuff of every[thing-one was in dis
array and lacked finished form / next someone [was bo
rn, he says, who bu[ilt and furnished
everything-one / next (he says) [w]ay was born, [and while w
ay was passing by, sign follow[ed] closely in understanding com
pliance / now way really is the beginning as it were, while si
gn (acts as the) end-completion (of extant possibility) /
after (sea mother) Thetis was
born, (way and sign, the) beginning and end-comp[l]etio[n thes]e
(two) of everything-one, w
ere bo[r]n / and indeed the everything-one has a nature-(from)-birth

(which is) [the sa]me as
the unwrought timberstuff of copper
(or: of all metals before iron: bronze, brass, etc.), while
Thetis (was) i[ts] artificer-shaper, and way and si
gn (worked as) beginning and end-completion /
(in this poem Alcman uses the form) *oll[d maan]*

───────

instead of the (usual word for) old man /
(he says) *and third shadowdarkness*

───────

because neither sun nor m
o]on had yet been born since (at that time)
t]he unwrought timberstuff (of everything-one)
was still unpart[e]d-unmingl[e]d / indeed
                    under-by-from . [.] . . w
ay and sign and shadowdark[ness] were born . / [*day*

───────

and moon and third shadowdarkness / the
flashings-sparklings-glancing glitterdartings (of stars?) /
day (was) not (born) all by herself but
(at the same time-by the same act) as (the) sun /
for previously shadowdarkness lived (all) alo
ne, but afterwards when he'd been part[e]d-mixedandmingl[e]d

FROM THE *HOMERIC ALLEGORIES*
OF HERACLITOS THE GRAMMARIAN

A Greek text by Heraclitos the Grammarian, c. 30 B.C.–
c. A.D. 14. Provenance unknown. Text: *Héraclite: Allégories
d'Homère* (Buffière, ed.), 62.

sometime long ago before the ForeMother set out the Wholes
and gave them roots

when what was not had not yet had its character struck
or else lay blanketed under mere-slime
since she had not picked out Types
to imprint her young impressionables
or driven a center spike deep into Earth her Wholes' vestal heart
spinning Sky on it to secure his swift changeless fruitful rush

when everything was   sunless desert   downcast soundless night
things-not-things   unfilled
by the still empty MotherTimberStuff
for this was a slack time her lovely bodyforms had yet to employ

then WorldMother Start worked everything into her fashion
drawing them for safety and health into her body
to give them birth
she bore the universe her beauty's/*cosmos* which is also order
unhooked earth from sky unfurled endless land and sea
untangling them from each other
for her self's adorning arranged 4 Rows
the 4 Roots that bear the Wholes
in fore-thought/clusters that re-produce
the well-turned features of her Nature

after she'd considered everything
before shuffling each into place
the god . . . since she had no clear choice
separated into shape her once aimless body . . .

DAMASCIUS, THE IRANIAN COSMOGONY

A Greek text by Damascius, c. A.D. 500, from an Iranian source, c. third century A.D. Text: Damascius, *De Principiis* (Ruelle, ed.).

everything you see   PLACE   or

TIME

which separate in Two
making a double pair

OROMESDES   who is   Light
Ahura-Mazda

AREIMANIOS   who is   Dark
Ariman

PLACE
Topos

————Zerauné akerené

TIME
Chronos

FROM THE 36TH *DISCOURSE*
OF DIO CHRYSOSTOM

A Greek text, c. first century A.D., taken from a Persian source
after the fifth century B.C. Text: Dio Chrysostom, *Discourses*
(H. Crosby, ed.), Vol. V.

Everybody knows the Sun has a chariot
            but what about Zeus's?
               his is much older
                yet not a word about it in Homer or Hesiod

      Zoroaster knew
             he had a song which he taught the Magi

                 alone on a mountain
               he lived in his love of wisdom

     then the mountain burned
              fire falling from the sky
                never stopping
          the shah and his court came to witness

the prophet stepped out of the sheath of flame unhurt
            "I'm all right
               you should be too
         burn food for the god who's come here"

      Zoroaster went into the world
            and lived with the Wise: the Magi
           whom he showed the demonic

they are not magicians as the Greeks say

        for Zeus they keep a team of Nisaean horses
          the best and biggest in Asia
         but for the Sun—just one horse

The Story of the Horses and the World

think the diacosm a 4 horse chariot drawn along a single road
by the highest driver who does   and   knows
no stopping no ending his driving
an eternal turning in time
Sun and Moon only partial to the whole
so people see them
but they're partials too
the diacosm's moving and circling
most never notice
because the struggle's so great

the four Horses

first: Aither

on the outside runs the longest track
big beautiful fast
Zeus's favorite
wings color of fire of spotless light
Sun Moon other stars piebalds on his hide
sparks in clusters flying rippling
in close night

some in formation
others off by themselves
dancing slapping against each other

loners: the planets
the troupes: constellations
figures schematic form patterns

second: Hera/Air

who obeys is gentle weak and slow
black
but bright where Sun strikes
otherwise in shadow
turns to find color

third: Poseidon/Water
                    slower than Hera

         once he came down   the poets say
                              his image Pegasos
                         hoof pawed earth a fountain leapt up
                         Spring Peirené at Corinth
                                   still there
                                         you can see it

fourth: Hestia/Earth
                         who does not move has no wings
              (don't ask me to explain
                              certain things just can't be
                    besides this is a story)

                    hitched to the chariot
                                   he stands still
                    chewing the iron bit
Hera and Poseidon bend toward him pushing and crowding
         but Aither farthest away
                              always rounds him first
                    while he holds steady as a turning post
                                        in the hippodrome

The Hebrew cosmogony of the J-E tradition, c. 2000–700 B.C.
Text: Kittel, *Biblia Hebraica,* Gen. 2.4b–.23.

When Yahweh of the gods was making earth and skies

> not even a wild bush existed on earth
> not even a wild grass had come up

> since Yahweh of the gods hadn't made rain on earth
> since no Landman was to work the earth

> water'd just gush from the earth
> and water 'cross the whole land

Yahweh of the gods shaped landman from lumps of land, and blew the soft-blowing wind of life into his nostrils. So then landman was breathing life. Then Yahweh of the gods planted a garden on a pleasant plain in the east, and put the landman he'd shaped there. Then Yahweh of the gods raised every tree worth looking at and worth eating from, and in the middle of the garden is the tree of immortality and the tree of knowing-what's-good-and-bad. A river comes up in the plain to water the garden, then splits into four branches: one of them is the Hopper, winding through all of the Havila country, where the gold is—good gold at that—and bdellium and lapis lazuli; the second river's name is Gusher—that's the one that winds all through the Kassite country; the name of the third river is Tigris, which runs east of Ashur; and the fourth is the Euphrates.

Anyway, Yahweh of the gods took landman and put him in the garden on the pleasant plain to work it and watch it. Then Yahweh of the gods commanded the landman: "You can eat from any of the trees of the garden except the tree of knowing-what's-good-and-bad. If you eat from that one, you're doomed from then on."

So then Yahweh of the gods said to himself, "It's not good landman being alone. I'll make him the right helper."

So
from the land
Yahweh of the gods shaped
all the wild animals
all the birds of the skies

Then he brought them to the landman to see what he'd call them. Whatever the landman called them is their name.

So
the landman gave names
to every bird of the skies
to every wild life

But he didn't find a fit helper for the landman. So Yahweh of the gods put the landman into a deep sleep. When he was asleep, he took one of his ribs then closed the flesh back up. Then Yahweh of the gods built the rib he'd taken from the landman into a woman, and brought her to the landman, who sang:

"That's the one
a bone from my bones
a flesh from my flesh

This one will be called woman
'Cause she's taken from a   man."

That's why a man'll leave his father and mother: to hang around his woman, because they're one flesh.

THE PHOENICIAN COSMOGONY
ACCORDING TO MOCHOS

The Phoenician cosmogony according to Mochos, a Greek text, c. A.D. 500; taken from a Phoenician source, c. ninth–eighth century B.C. (after Sanchuniathon). Text: Damascius, *De Principiis* (Ruelle, ed.).

he-Fire she-Air

their son ⎧'OLAM
⎩Chronos

who makes love to himself

his son ⎧CHUSOROS the Egg-Opener
⎩[Phanes?]

next Egg

below them the Winds in degree

Wind: Ruaḥ

Winds: ⎧LIPS and ⎧NOTOS
⎩Libyan ⎩["fatherless"?]

Egg is ⎧SKY
⎩Uranos

for when Egg hatched

the half shells became   sky and earth

From the Phoenician city of Sidon, a Greek text, c. A.D. 500, taken from a Greek source, Eudemos (fourth century B.C.) reporting a Phoenician source from the eighth–seventh century B.C. Text: Damascius, *De Principiis* (Ruelle, ed.). ". . ." denotes words omitted.

{ CHRONOS
{ 'Olam

then { POTHOS   and   { OMICLÉ
{ Desire   { Darkness

from these two

the first Two:

he-Fire
she-Breath

. . .

from the first Two mixing and mingling: { OTÜS
{ Egg

Fragment 57 from *Hypsipylé,* a lost play by Euripides, contains one of the oldest of the Orphic cosmogonies, c. 1000 B.C. Text: Kern, *Orphicorum Fragmenta* #2. "[. . .]" denotes words supplied.

. . . [Night]

you who rule the gods

[mother of] {LOVE the unseen demanding {LIGHT
           {Eros   {[Phanes?]

child you bore first to fireair . . .

THE COSMIC OUTLINE OF ACUSILAUS

This cosmological summary, c. A.D. 500, was abstracted from the works of the Greek poet Acusilaus, c. seventh–sixth century B.C. Text: Damascius, *De Principiis* (Ruelle, ed.).

first
Gap the unknown
then

Erebos
he
bounded

Night
she
boundless

their
children:
Aither
Eros
Metis

their
children's
children:
the other gods

FRAGMENTS FROM EPIMENIDES,
THE *BIRTH OF THE GODS* OR *ORACLES*

This Greek text by Epimenides dates from the sixth century B.C. It contains an Orphic cosmology which goes back probably to at least the seventh or eighth century B.C. Text: in Diels-Kranz, *Die Fragmente der Vorsokratiker*, Vol. 1. "———" divides the fragments. "(. . .)" denotes a possibly spurious fragment.

Moon of lovely hair my mother
              in my house sharing the smoke

      I shuddered and shook the lion
      I met in Nemea and choked
            for Hera

———

first FireAir and Night
          then Pit

       three from two
      mixing and mingling

———

            two from three
              mixing and mingling
                 { TITANS
                 { tighteners
      stretching from top to bottom
              beginning to end

      coming together
           egg
      one
      everyone

———

                    I have no stories about what will be
                only what was and then I speak in "if's"

————

there is no navel set in the middle of earth and sea
                                        anchoring the cord
                    or "if" so
                    the gods see it
                            we don't

————

(⎰DIO's ⎰KOUROI   were man and woman
  ⎱Zeus' ⎱lads

                                    he   timemaker   one

                                    she   earth   two

                        from one and two every number

                                    lives and breathes)

EURIPIDES,

FRAGMENT 6 OF THE *MELANIPPÉ*

This Greek text from a lost play by Euripides dates from the late fifth century B.C. Text: Nauck, *Tragicorum Graecorum Fragmenta.*

this is not my story
but one my mother tells

once Sky and Earth were one
then they split in   two

father and mother of all

brought into light
trees
birds
beasts
fish in the sea
race of living men

JUSTIN, *BARUCH*

This Greek text, c. first century A.D., is probably a condensed translation of Justin's Hebrew or Aramaic original, c. A.D. 40–70. Text: Hippolytus, *Refutatio* (Philosophumenon), ed. Wendland.

what eye has not seen
or ear heard
what has not yet entered heart

now hush
give the gift
of tongue

Heracles Mel-kart drove Geryon's cattle into Scythia
fell asleep in the desert
woke up   horse gone   cattle too
look   search
found SnakeWoman
from cunt on up a maiden girl
but beware the serpent tail below
"seen my horse?"
"make me"
does so: throws   3 kids in her bag/behind/cunt centering her
got his horse and cattle back
left

that's the world being laid out

3 beginners

Yahweh Good Pap Priapos Straight Cock Herding Lady's Thing
who sees what will be before it is

Elohim the FatherorMother
who can't see this
but invisibly
is allowed to father himself everywhere

Eden Israel SnakeWoman
who knows as little as FatherorMother
but can she feel!
thinking twice
two body
cunt up woman
cunt down snake

they are the roots the fountains
without &
thanks to whom nothing everything the way it is
and continually being made up and taken away

FatherorMother looked at Eden half woman Israel the rest snake
"got to have her"

"Elohim
I want you too
just as much
more maybe"

bed

love

fuck

children
the 12 father's angels

Michael Amen
(*these things says the Amen,
the faithful and true witness
the beginning of the creation of God*)
Baruch Gabriel Esaddaios . . .

the 12 mother's angels

Babel Achamoth Naas Baal Belias Satan Sael
Adonaios Leviathon Pharaoh Carcomenos Lathen

the father's are Elohim's   the mother's Eden Israel's

all of them in the Paradise
the Lord God planted
east of Eden
turned toward her face
so she could see it
and see her angel children

the trees of the garden these angels
to say one word for another
the trees are angels

tree of life : Baruch
tree of knowledge of good and bad : Serpent Naas

Paradise is made of the married joy of Elohim and Eden
where their angels enroot earth's loveliest plots

now earth is Eden Israel but not the snake torso
from cunt above groin in wife body
gentle and mild to gaze at
she made man out of her dirt meat

out of snake springs below cunt she took wild beasts animal creation

men and women chain in flesh the love of FatherorMother and Earth

"take my windair" she says to Adam
"my fire" he says   to him

"I give her airwind
my picture cuts her size" :
Eden to Eve

"give her my fire" said   Elohim

Adam   signed sealed delivered the covenant still endures
and Eve:
"we are one   soul and spirit
and between you"

       "multiply and divide
           make up by fucking
                the numbers of the dead
          until they even out the living"

Eden Israel dowered her strength on Elohim
                 that's why brides give dowries
          because what Eden did is law

mother's angels 4 groups of 3
        that makes four beginners
                each   called a river of Paradise
                  Phison Gehon Tigris Euphrates
hold hands and run the world in Eden's name
        dancing in a circle
                never in one place too long
                    fixing time to change
           appointed places
            their homes

where Phison is hunger is and pain and woe
        what a cheap squad
            you are, Phison

to each part of the four according to their power and nature
        bad times
        rotten plagues

from their bossing and mixing/mingling
           flood rivers
        currents careers
           what Eden wants
      no stop for breath just keep it up lady
        people have to be bad
             it's her way
       there's evil in the world

Elohim had fixed up Earth for his "little" garden
        but now time for something else
       "will go up into the sky
         make sure nothing's left out"

father's angels went along

up   up

"goodbye Eden"
"I am earth I can't leave here"
"right—catch you later"

Elohim at the ceiling of sky saw a light above the light he gave
"open the gates for me to know my lord for I thought I was"
and the light said
"this is the gate of the Lord which the righteous shall enter"
    the gate opened up
Elohim went in
          his angels did not
to Good Dad Cock
              saw *what eye has not seen or ear heard*
                    what has not yet entered heart

Yahweh said
      "sit at my right hand"

Elohim asked
          "Lord let me overturn the world I made
              my fire is chained to men to empty skies"
"no bad now
          you are with me
                  you and Eden did the world from married joy
                        let her own it as she wants to
                                      and no longer—
                    you stay with me"

Eden Elohim's desert
          felt love die when he went away
                      tears in her eyes
                              put mother's angels on her side
dress up time for mother whore nature earth
cheap green leaf Eden sleeve
couched open cunt in the universe
draw Elohim down to her with sloe-eyed winks?
her idea
          hasn't worked yet

Elohim mastered by Papa Cock
        never came back

Eden told Babel Aphrodite
      "make the quimin liars
           undo their wounds
              pinch out their husbands' Elohim fire
                he divorced me
        make his flame in men go dead
            they not know love
              death heavy in the heart
            then feeling ugly
        discover inside the pain he burns me with
        driven from their women by adultery and deceit
           hurt as I was hurt by FatherorMother"
she made Naas strong to blind the Elohim in men
to strike at him through them
      for leaving his qwyf Earth voiding his promise to her

because of this he sent down Baruch
to tend his fire in everyone men and women

Baruch in the midst of the angels of Eden (FAILURE)
           in the midst of paradise park
              (for the garden is the angels
                  where he stood)
said to Adam
     "eat the fruits of all the trees of paradise
       except the tree Naas who knows right from wrong
      listen to the 11 angels of Eden
        for they feel
      but are innocent of law
        of going against it and breaking it
          but not Naas
            don't hear him"

     cushioning her slice Naas knew Eve
        gave her lie
        made her fig skirts of shame
      he broke the knotty rose in Adam's anus jerked
         and left his water there

quimin fucking for any reason
men holing men
Naas' work
        if you can get it

Elohim sets out good from bad
                he the single of yes and no
on Cock Dad's right
        shows people the way to him

                but by turning out Eden
                        he began evil
                                in the fire
                                        he laid in us

next he sent Baruch to Moses (FAILURE)
                his person when he talked to
                                the children of Israel
                        to bend them to Yahweh
        Naas swam thru Eden's airwind
                        squirmed inside Moses and his chosen
                                to sod shut the light of Baruch's words
                        so they heard him only

    (airwind is Eden fighting fire Elohim fighting back
    inside
    man or woman   doesn't matter)

Baruch to Prophets (FAILURE)
                to warn Elohim in everyone
                        "avoid Eden
                                and the lie of the world she gives
                        just as FatherorMother did"

Naas enjoyed the Prophets ass backwards
sexed them away from Elohim
supposing Eden's airwind in them
they did not choose
Baruch's words Elohim's laws

sent Heracles Mel-kart (FAILURE)
gentile prophet   hooded cock head
"break the 12 mother's angels
set me free"

the 12 Labors he suffered—Lion Hydra Boar etc.:
goy names borrowed and changed from the energy
of Eden's messengers

looked like he cracked them down   he'd won
then Omphalé robed in her sleek skin body
peeled his cock lace back
soothing him of strength
of Baruch's word
Elohim's issue

what did he get instead?
an envelope of flesh
a narrow slot
run by Eden the power below
Heracles Mel-kart your words did not come true
your deeds still need doing

Baruch to Nazareth (AN OUTCOME?)
when Herod was king
to Jesus son of Joseph and Mary
12 years old
tending sheep

told him the story of the world which is just the story
          of Eden and Elohim
        marrying and divorcing

and about whatever else looked toward being born and being true
       "Naas rammed up the ass
           of every prophet before you
      licked away their delight in Daddy Cock

        Jesus Man Son don't let him snake his ways
              through the bowels of your love
      tell everybody of FatherorMother
               and Yahweh his lord
        then go on up
           sit beside Elohim my father"

true to Baruch Jesus made the news

      which turned Naas rampant
         "that boy close his shit gate to me?
           spread him on the cross
              in front of me
      we'll see who's coming who's going"

on the withered tree of Naas Jesus abandoned Eden's body
          going up to Good Dad
        last words : "woman, you have your son"
          the child born of earth must die in her

Jesus gave his fire back to Cock Dad
and went to him to Priapos
who brought out whatever is before it was
fashioning out of his body from the shapes of his mind
that's why you see terminals of him in every temple
that everything that is born loves
his roadside stubs balance sweet fruit on their glans
for   he shepherded birth
        before earth womb bulged

when the swan nests on Leda
   that's Elohim buttering Israel
when the eagle rears up Ganymede
    Naas worms Adam
when the gold storms Danaë's snatch
     golden Elohim floors black Eden's tubes

and so through the stories of instruction
(when Heracles Mel-kart drove Geryon's cattle through Scythia
   he met
     . . . the snake woman in the desert
      . . . how the world was fathered
       . . . Naas bowing his head
         clamps tail between teeth)

hear, sky
listen, earth
the Lord speaks
   fire of Elohim is inside
   Earth's windair the soul right alongside
Baruch is your Lord

Eden Israel married and divorced Elohim
   who said
  "Israel did not know me
    if she did
     that I am with Yahweh Straight Cock
  she would not have struck out in mother's ignorance
     at my fire in mankind"

   the Lord has sworn and will not repent

    so now take the Oath of Baruch

  "I swear by Goad Priapos who is above all
  to guard these Secrets
  and tell them to no one
  I promise not to fall back
  from Man Cock to Wom(b)man Cunt"

then you will see what *eye has not seen or ear heard*
                              what has not yet entered heart
and drink from *welling water springing up into everlasting life*
in the basin of the fountain of live bubbling water

                for water has been taken from water
                        brack fish water below the arched sky
        swilling   in Eden's cunt
            the siren   allure ring   in her snaker tress
                        washes earth and animal men
                fresh life water above the blue groined heaven
                        the light-flecked come of Cock Papa
            dyes pale bright the living
                    the fire sky lonely who ditched   their quimin

Elohim washes here
                and having washed *did not repent*

go take a wife of whoredoms
for earth has done great whoredoms
departing from the Lord

Eden empties Elohim
                that is the whole Secret
                    now watch out for
                                Serpent Naas
                    don't let him get
                            behind you

Elemental Creation

III. DIVIDING

Autonomic and Aliyan Texts

B. ALIYAN TEXTS

Akkadian text with other Semitic styles and attitudes, c. 1500 B.C. Texts: Labat, *Le poème babylonien de la création;* Lambert, *Enuma elish;* Landsberger and Wilson, "Tablet V of enuma eliš," *Journal for Near Eastern Studies #20.*

When sky above had no name
    earth beneath no given name

⎰ APSU   the first   their seeder
⎱ Deepwater
⎰ TIAMAT
⎱ Saltsea their mother   who bore them
                      mixed waters

Before pasture held together
    thicket be found
no gods being
no names for them
no plans

the gods were shaped inside them

LAḪMU AND LAḪAMU were brought out
                  named
while they grew
    became great
⎰ ANŠAR and ⎰ KIŠAR were shaped
⎱ Skyline   ⎱ Earthline   much greater
       made the days long
       added the years

⎰ ANU was their son
⎱ Sky   their rival
⎰ ANŠAR made his first son ⎰ ANU his equal
⎱ Skyline   ⎱ Sky

and {ANU / Sky} got {NUDIMMUD / Manmaker / (EA)} equal

{NUDIMMUD / Manmaker / (EA)}   his fathers' boss

                    wide wise

                          full knowing

stronger than {ANŠAR / Skyline his father}   strong

no equal among his brother gods

The godbrothers   together

stormed in {TIAMAT / Saltsea}

stirred up {TIAMAT / Saltsea} 's guts

rushing at the walls

Not {APSU / Deepwater} hush their noise

{TIAMAT / Saltsea} struck dumb

They did bad things to her

    acted badly, childishly

until {APSU / Deepwater}   seeder of great gods

              called up {MUMMU / Speaker:}

{MUMMU / "Speaker   messenger   makes my liver happy

                come!   {TIAMAT

                    Let's go see {Saltsea."}

They went   {TIAMAT

    sat down in front of {Saltsea}

    (talk about plans for their first-born gods):

$\left\{\begin{array}{l}\text{APSU}\\\text{Deepwater}\end{array}\right.$ opened his mouth   said

to $\left\{\begin{array}{l}\text{TIAMAT}\\\text{Saltsea}\end{array}\right.$ said loud:

"The way they act makes me sick:
during the day   no rest
at night   no sleep

I'll destroy them!
     stop their doings!
It'll be quiet again   we can sleep"

When $\left\{\begin{array}{l}\text{TIAMAT}\\\text{Saltsea}\end{array}\right.$ heard this

                         she stormed
                         yelled at her husband
                         was sick
                         alone:

          "Wipe out what we made?!

          The way they act *is* a pain
                         but let's wait"

$\left\{\begin{array}{l}\text{MUMMU}\\\text{Speaker answered}\end{array}\right.$ advising $\left\{\begin{array}{l}\text{APSU}\\\text{Deepwater:}\end{array}\right.$ $\left\{\begin{array}{l}\text{MUMMU}\\\text{Speaker's}\\\text{ill-meant}\end{array}\right.$
                         bad advice

"Go on!
          Put an end to their impertinence
                              then
rest   during the day
sleep   at night"

When $\left\{\begin{array}{l}\text{APSU}\\\text{Deepwater}\end{array}\right.$ heard him

                         his face gleamed
                              for the hurts planned
                              against his godsons

hugged $\left\{\begin{array}{l}\text{MUMMU}\\\text{Speaker}\end{array}\right.$
set him in his lap
kissed him

What they planned in conference was repeated
to their firstborn godsons
They wept
     milled around   distressed
    kept silence

$\left\{\begin{array}{l}\text{EA}\\\text{Waterhome}\end{array}\right.$ most understanding
                       skillful
                       wise
                       knowing all
                                  saw through the plot

  came up with a plan   made it up
crafted his spell   pure and mastering
made it sound the water
                 where slept $\left\{\begin{array}{l}\text{APSU}\\\text{Deepwater well}\end{array}\right.$
poured more sleep
stretched him out
soaked him with sleep

Counsel $\left\{\begin{array}{l}\text{MUMMU}\\\text{Speaker}\end{array}\right.$ stuck still

$\left\{\begin{array}{l}\text{APSU}\\\text{Deepwater's belt}\end{array}\right.$ crown   aura
he   took off   tore away   ripped off
         tied up $\left\{\begin{array}{l}\text{APSU}\\\text{Deepwater}\end{array}\right.$ killed him
         tied up $\left\{\begin{array}{l}\text{MUMMU}\\\text{Speaker}\end{array}\right.$ shut him up

Found a house in ⎰APSU
              ⎱Deepwater
led off ⎰MUMMU by the nose
      ⎱Speaker

After whipping his enemies   treading them
did ⎰EA   rest   sureset victor
   ⎱Waterhome
inside his holy home in deep peace

called it the Apsu
woven reed cult hut he founded

LAḪMU AND LAḪAMU
EA   and DAMKINNA
Waterhome and Earthandskylady   lived there
in greatness
in the shrine of fate
                    lodge of divine order

Wisest wise   ⎧MARDUK   god was conceived
                     ⎨Sunchild
                     ⎩godsage

                           ⎰MARDUK
in side the Apsu   ⎱Sunchild born
in side godly Apsu   ⎰MARDUK born
                           ⎱Sunchild

⎰EA   his father   fathered him
⎱Waterhome
⎰DAMKINNA
⎱Earthandskylady   his mother   brought him out

goddess' tit he sucked
nurse nursed him full of fear

build seduced   raised eye flashed
manly at birth   mighty from the start

When ⌈EA   his father
    ⌊Waterhome   who fathered him
                        saw him

he became happy
        laughed
             heart full of joy

He polished him up
    doubled his godness   raised above gods':

his lines   unknowable
              fine-made
              unthinkable
              unseeable:
              fourfold eye
              fourfold ear

              lips moved   fire flashed
              fourfold   huge eared
              samenumber eyes   saw all
              highest god   tallest tall
              hugest limbs   highest height

"My son   my son!
Sunchild   skySun!"

                        Dressed in 10 gods' aura
                           strongest
                           lightning charged

Then
⌈ANU
⌊Sky   bears the fourwinds
                  in front   the allwind the whirlwind
                       made waves   ⌈TIAMAT
                       stirring stirring the⌊Saltsea
    ⌈TIAMAT
The⌊Saltsea   troubled
                  comings and goings   day and night
                  the gods harassed again

the gods in their hearts plot evil
they   brothers   to ⎰TIAMAT
                      ⎱Saltsea:

"When they killed ⎰APSU
                   ⎱Deepwater your lover
      you did not go with him   but sat still

"Now *he*'s made the terror wind
          your belly's disturbed   *we* can't sleep

⎰ "APSU
⎱ Deepwater be in your heart
⎰ MUMMU
⎱ Speaker   caught   you live   alone
                              turn along
                              don't love us

"Our eyes droop   burn
                      all the time
     We want sleep
     Fight!   and Revenge!
     Make them ghosts!"

⎰TIAMAT
⎱Saltsea   heard   brightened god
           said   "Advice you've given
                    Let's make stormmonsters
                             gods among them
                    All battle against gods!"

They troop to her
      surround ⎰TIAMAT
               ⎱Saltsea

                    fiercely scheming   day and night
          raise the battle   growling roaring
                        forming fuming

Mother ⎡ ḪUBUR
⎨ undariver
⎣ (TIAMAT)   all things molder

                   makes weapons
                      none like them

                  bears dragons
                    sharptoothed
                    merciless fangs

                  fills their bodies
                    poison not blood

                  clothes roaring dragons
                    with dread
                       splendor
                  makes them gods

      (whoever sees them dies despairing
        once they rear up they never back down)

She raised up:
          a bašmu-dragon
          a mušḫuššu-snake
          a laḫamu-monster
          a Grand Lion
          a Mad Dog
          a Man-scorpion
          Howling winds
          a Man-fish
          a Bison

                    They carry unstoppable arms
                      are fearless
                  her order so powerful
                      irresistible

She made 11 monsters   these
and from the gods   the firstborn
               surrounding her
                    raised up ⎡ KINGU
                            ⎣ land from them all
               greatened him:

The first rank   the battle group leader
the arms raiser   the charger to war
the commander of the troops
she handed him   seating him in Council

"I've said the spell for you
        raised you in God Assembly
        filled your hand potent
                                over all the gods
   Rise! you my mate   my only
                        your name
                                over all the ⌠ANUNNAKI
                                             ⌊sky and earthgods"

She gave him the Tablets of Fate
                                hung them on his chest:
"So   your command not to be changed
        your word   fixed"

When ⌠KINGU   was over all
     ⌊land   was as ⌠ANU
                      ⌊Sky   he set the fates for his sons
                                                the gods:

"Words of your mouths douse the fire
  Mighty so in war
                shaking very Might"

COLOPHON TO TABLET 1   *First tablet of enuma*
eliš written according to the original   *the tablet of Nabu-*
balat-su-iqbi   son of Na'id-Marduk   *by the hand of Nabu-*
balat-su-iqbi   son of Na'id-Marduk

Tablet I of enuma eliš after . . . *a copy from Babylon writ-*
ten according to the original   the tablet of Nabu-musetiq-
umi son of . . . *who fears Marduk and Ṣarpanitum   and*
did it not in fraud nor turning aside from the way . . . *month*
of Ayyar   9th day   27th year of Darius

When $\begin{cases} \text{TIAMAT} \\ \text{Saltsea'd made her work strong} \end{cases}$

　　　　　raised her offspring to battle against the gods
　　　　　did evil to revenge $\begin{cases} \text{APSU} \\ \text{Deepwater} \end{cases}$

It was told to $\begin{cases} \text{EA} \\ \text{Waterhome} \end{cases}$

Hearing　　$\begin{cases} \text{EA} \\ \text{Waterhome} \end{cases}$

　　　　　　　stilled in black quiet　wordless

When he'd thought　　his anger ebbed
　　he went up　　to his father　$\begin{cases} \text{ANŠAR who fathered him} \\ \text{Skyline} \end{cases}$

　　　told what $\begin{cases} \text{TIAMAT planned:} \\ \text{Saltsea} \end{cases}$

"My father　　$\begin{cases} \text{TIAMAT} \\ \text{Saltsea} \end{cases}$ mothered us　　hates us

　　　　　　　　　　　　　　　calls a troop
　　　　　　　　　　　　　　　mad　boils
　all gods around her　　those you made too　　around her

They　troop　to　her
　　　surround $\begin{cases} \text{TIAMAT} \\ \text{Saltsea} \end{cases}$

　　　　　　　fiercely scheming　day and night
　　raise the battle　　growling　roaring
　　　　　　　forming　fuming

Mother ⌠ḪUBUR
    ⎰undariver
    ⌡(TIAMAT)   all things molder

                makes weapons
                   none like them

                bears dragons
                   sharptoothed
                    merciless fangs

                fills their bodies
                   poison not blood

                clothes roaring dragons
                with dread
                     splendor
                makes them gods

    (whoever sees them dies despairing
      once they rear up they never back down)

She raised up:
              a bašmu-dragon
              a mušḫuššu-snake
              a laḫamu-monster
              a Grand Lion
              a Mad Dog
              a Man-scorpion
              Howling winds
              a Man-fish
              a Bison

                   They carry unstoppable arms
                     are fearless
                 her order so powerful
                     irresistible

She made 11 monsters these
and from the gods   the firstborn
                  surrounding her

      raised up ⌠KINGU
              ⌡land   from them all
      greatened him:

The first rank   the battle group leader
the arms raiser   the charger to war
the commander of the troops
she handed him   seating him in Council

'I've said the spell for you
      raised you in God Assembly
      filled your hand potent
                        over all the gods
Rise!   you my mate   my only
                  your name
                        over all the ⎧ANUNNAKI
                                      ⎩sky and earthgods'

She gave him the Tablets of Fate
                        hung them on his chest:
'So   your command   not to be changed
      your word   fixed'

When ⎧KINGU   was over all
      ⎩land   was as ⎧ANU
                      ⎩Sky   he set the fates for the gods his sons:
'Words of your mouths douse the fire
Mighty so in war
                  shaking very Might' "

⎧ANŠAR   heard   how ⎧TIAMAT   stormed
⎩Skyline   ⎩Saltsea
            beat at his groin
            bit his lips
                  heart full of dread
                  spirit worried
            choked his cries:
                        ". . . to battle
                        You too must carry the arms you've made
      You've killed   ⎧MUMMU   ⎧APSU
                      ⎩Speaker   ⎩Deepwater
            now ⎧KINGU
                ⎩land   marches before her"

{ NUDIMMUD
{ Manmaker
{ (EA)   answered . . . . .

    { ANŠAR   { ANU
So { Skyline to { Sky   his son   called

                  said this
                  full of wrath:

"Here is one powerful   my hero
  strength beyond   . . .
attack invincible   Go to { TIAMAT
                    { Saltsea   See her
so her anger be quieted
   her heart opened

If she will not heed your word
say it is our word   to still her"

When he'd heard his father's   { ANŠAR
                           { Skyline's order
he headed for her   along the way
                       but
when he saw the battle order of { TIAMAT
                         { Saltsea
he did not dare see her
   turned back to his father   { ANŠAR
                       { Skyline
   cried what he had to say to   { TIAMAT
                        { Saltsea:

"My hand too weak
          to still you"

{ ANŠAR
{ Skyline   fell silent
            stared in the dirt

                              mumbling
                              head shaking

The ⌠ANUNNAKI   in Assembly   drew together
    ⌡sky and earthgods   lips sealed
                                  so silent stayed

                         No god would come at ⌠TIAMAT
                                              ⌡Saltsea
                         Facing ⌠TIAMAT
                                ⌡Saltsea none departs alive

The god ⌠ANŠAR   father of the gods
         ⌡Skyline   lifts himself   in splendor
                                     gathers his wits
                                     says to the ⌠ANUNNAKI
                                                  ⌡sky and earthgods

"Whose strength is strong
                    will stand for his father
                    smash this war:

                                   ⌠MARDUK
                                   ⌡Sunchild   hero"

So then ⌠EA   ⌠MARDUK
        ⌡Waterhome called ⌡Sunchild   to his place

When he came he spoke his heart:

⌠"MARDUK
⌡ Sunchild   a plan   hear your father
   My son   ease my heart

   Go to ⌠ANŠAR
          ⌡Skyline   as to war   straight
   Stand right up!
   Say!
       Seeing you he will be at ease"

The ⎧bel
　　⎨lord
　　⎩(MARDUK) rejoiced at his father's word
　　　　　　　drew near　　　stood at ⎧ANŠAR
　　　　　　　　　　　　　　　　　　 ⎩Skyline

⎧ANŠAR
⎩Skyline looked on him　　his heart stuffed with joy
　　　　kissed his lips　　drove off fear

⎧"ANŠAR　　　not dumb
⎩Skyline　　　open your lips
　I bring you full heart
⎧ANŠAR　　　not dumb
⎩Skyline　　　open your lips
　I bring you full heart

What man try you in battle?
A woman　⎧TIAMAT　　marches on you
　　　　　⎩Saltsea
My father　my maker　be happy　relax
Soon enough your feet on ⎧TIAMAT 's neck!
　　　　　　　　　　　　 ⎩Saltsea
My father　my maker　be happy　relax
Soon enough your feet on ⎧TIAMAT
　　　　　　　　　　　　 ⎩Saltsea's neck!"

"My son　　know all wisdom
　still ⎧TIAMAT
　　　　⎩Saltsea　　by your bright word!

Drive hard the storm car!

Not her helpers hold you back
drive them back!"

The ⎧bel　　　　　rejoiced at his father's word
　　⎨lord　　　　　heart bright
　　⎩(MARDUK)　said to his father:

<pre>
 ⌈"Bel   of the gods   Fate of the great gods
 ⎨ lord
 ⌊ (ANŠAR)
   if I be your avenger
      beat ⌈TIAMAT
           ⌊Saltsea
   save your lives
</pre>

                           call Assembly
                           make my fate all potent!
                           Fate it!
                           in the ⌈UPŠUKINNA   sit happy
                                  ⌊Fates' hall
                           my word   I set Fate   like you
                           Unchangeable all I make
                           fixed   set   my lips command"

COLOPHON TO TABLET II   *Tablet II of enuma*
eliš   after the text of the tablet . . .   a copy from Assur

---

COLOPHON TO (another) TABLET II   *Written*
according to the original   the tablet of Nabu-aḫē-iddin
son of Eṭir-bel   son of the priest of Maš   no departure
from the way   no blame

ANŠAR   opens his mouth
Skyline   says to KAKA   his speaker   these words:

"Speaker KAKA   cheers my heart
 I send you to LAḪMU and LAḪAMU

 You can make points   can chatter

 Bring the gods   my fathers   to me
       all the gods   come here together
                         talk with each other
                         sit at table
                         eat bread
                         drink wine

for {MARDUK
   {Sunchild   avenger fix fate

Go on KAKA   when before them   say them   I say:
{'ANŠAR   your son   sends me to you
{ Skyline   commands me say his heart word:

{"TIAMAT   mothered us
{ Saltsea   hates us   calls a troop
                                                     mad   boils
all gods around her   those you made too   around her
They troop to her
        surround {TIAMAT
                 {Saltsea
                          fiercely scheming   day and night
        raise the battle   growling   roaring
                                forming   fuming

Mother {ḤUBUR
       {undariver   all things molder
       {(TIAMAT)   makes weapons
                                                   none like them
                                           bears dragons
                                                   sharptoothed
                                                   merciless fangs
                                           fills their bodies
                                                   poison not blood
                                           clothes roaring dragons
                                                   with dread
                                                       splendor
                                           makes them gods

        (whoever sees them dies despairing
         once they rear up they never back down)

She raised up:

      a bašmu-dragon
      a mušḫuššu-snake
      a laḫamu-monster
      a Grand Lion
      a Mad Dog
      a Man-scorpion
      Howling winds
      a Man-fish
      a Bison

              They carry unstoppable arms
                  are fearless

             Her order   so powerful
                   irresistible

She made 11 monsters   these
and from the gods   the firstborn   surrounding her
           raised up {KINGU
                 {land   from them all
           greatened him:
The first rank   the battle group leader
the arms raiser   the charger to war
the commander of the troops
she handed him   seating him in Council:

'I've said the spell for you
    raised you in God Assembly
    filled your hand potent
                over all the gods

Rise   you my mate   my only
             your name
                over all the {ANUNNAKI
                      {sky and earthgods'

She gave him the Tablets of Fate
              hung them on his chest:

'So   your command   not to be changed
       your word   fixed'

When ⎰KINGU   was over all
　　⎱land   was as ⎰ANU
　　　　　　　　　　　⎱Sky   he set the fates for the gods
　　　　　　　　　　　　　　　　　　　　his sons:

'Words of your mouths   douse the fire
 Mighty so in war
　　　　　　　　　shaking very Might!'

I sent ⎰ANU
　　　⎱Sky   could not face her
　　　⎰NUDIMMUD
　　　⎨Manmaker
　　　⎩(EA)   feared   turned back

　　　⎰MARDUK
　　　⎱Sunchild   stood out   wisest wise   your son
　　　　　　　　　made   to go face ⎰TIAMAT
　　　　　　　　　　　　　　　　　⎱Saltsea

　　　　　　　　　opens mouth   says to me:

'If I be your avenger
　　　beat ⎰TIAMAT
　　　　　⎱Saltsea
　　　save your lives

　　　　　　　　　　call Assembly
　　　　　　　　　　make my fate all potent!
　　　　　　　　　　Fate it!

　　　　　　　　　　　In ⎰UPŠUKINNA   sit happy
　　　　　　　　　　　　⎱Fates' hall
　　　　　　　　　　　　my word   I set fate   like you
　　　　　　　　　　　　Unchangeable all I make
　　　　　　　　　　　　fixed   set   my lips' command'

Hurry here   fix him fast your fates
He will face your mighty enemy" ' "

Then KAKA left   made his way
                before LAḤMU and LAḤAMU the gods his fathers
                        fell down
                        kissed the ground at their feet
                        bowing deep
                        said to them:

{ "ANŠAR   your son   sends me to you
{ Skyline   commands me say his heart word:

{ 'TIAMAT   mothered us
{ Saltsea   hates us   calls a troop
                                    mad   boils
all gods around her   those you made too   around her
They troop to her
        surround { TIAMAT
                 { Saltsea

                        fiercely scheming   day and night
        raise the battle   growling   roaring
                        forming   fuming

Mother { ḪUBUR
       { undariver   all things molder
       { (TIAMAT)   makes weapons
                                none like them
                        bears dragons
                                sharptoothed
                                merciless fangs
                        fills their bodies
                                poison not blood
                        clothes roaring dragons
                                with dread
                                        splendor
                        makes them gods

        (whoever sees them dies despairing
        once they rear up they never back down)

She raised up:
                a bašmu-dragon

                a mušḫuššu-snake
                a laḫamu-monster
                a Grand Lion
                a Mad Dog
                a Man-scorpion
                Howling winds
                a Man-fish
                a Bison

                                    They carry unstoppable arms
                                        are fearless

                                    Her order   so powerful
                                                irresistible

She made 11 monsters   these
    and from the gods   the firstborn   surrounding her
                    raised up   KINGU
                            land   from them all
                    greatened him:
the first rank   the battle group leader
the arms raiser   the charger to war
the commander of the troops
she handed him   seating him in Council:

"I've said the spell for you
        raised you in God Assembly
        filled your hand potent
                            over all the gods

Rise!   you my mate   my only
                        your name
                            over all the ⎰ANUNNAKI
                                         ⎱sky and earthgods"

She gave him the Tablets of Fate
                            hung them on his chest:

"So   your command   not to be changed
        your word   fixed"

When KINGU was over all
      land   was as ⌠ANU
              ⌡Sky
   he set the fates for the gods   his sons:
"Words of your mouths   douse the fire
Mighty so in war
              shaking very Might!"

I sent ⌠ANU
     ⌡Sky   could not face her
    ⌠NUDIMMUD
    ⟨Manmaker
    ⌡(EA)   feared   turned back
    ⌠MARDUK
    ⌡Sunchild   stood out   wisest wise   your son
                 made to go face ⌠TIAMAT
                           ⌡Saltsea
        opens mouth   says to me:
"If I be your avenger
    beat ⌠TIAMAT
        ⌡Saltsea
    save your lives
                    call Assembly
                    make my fate all potent
                    Fate it!
               In ⌠UPŠUKINNA   sit happy
                 ⌡Fates' hall
               my word   I set fate   like you
               Unchangeable all I make
               fixed   set   my lips' command"
Hurry here   fix him fast your fates
He will face your mighty enemy' "

When LAḪMU and LAḪAMU   heard   shrieked
  ⌠IGIGI
  ⌡heavenly gods   all   cried hard:
"What has come change   she make this so!?
  We   we don't know ways of ⌠TIAMAT
                           ⌡Saltsea"

Then they gather   go
all great gods   fate fixers

come in to $\left\{\begin{array}{l}\text{ANŠAR}\\\text{Skyline}\end{array}\right.$

fill the $\left\{\begin{array}{l}\text{UPŠUKINNA}\\\text{Fates' hall}\end{array}\right.$

kiss each other
hold Assembly
talk to each other
seat for feast
eat bread
drink wine
pour sweet wine in their cups
drinking tubes
wet with liquor
bodies heavy
drink drink
sweet heaviness through them
fix fate for $\left\{\begin{array}{l}\text{MARDUK}\\\text{Sunchild their avenger}\end{array}\right.$

TABLET III ENDS

---

make him a great throne
He sits in face his fathers   for speaking:

"You sure most heavy honor   among great gods
your fate unequal
your word $\left\{\begin{array}{l}\text{ANU}\\\text{Sky}\end{array}\right.$

$\left\{\begin{array}{l}\text{MARDUK}\\\text{Sunchild}\end{array}\right.$ most heavy honor   among great gods
your fate unequal
your word $\left\{\begin{array}{l}\text{ANU}\\\text{Sky}\end{array}\right.$

From now your word   unchangeable
        in your hand   lifting   lowering
                   unshaking
      your word
      your word   firm

No god cross your bounds

Support need god chambers
their sure chambers   your chamber

{ MARDUK
  Sunchild   our avenger
we give you reign   over all
Take place in Assembly
your word   here   rule
your weapons   invincible
                       wreck your enemies

{ BEL
 Lord
 (MARDUK)   Live your faithful!
                Die the god plots you ill!"

They extend a piece of cloth
    say to { MARDUK
            Sunchild   their firstborn:

{ "BEL
  Lord   your word first among gods
           'Make' 'Unmake'   so it is

    Open your mouth   cloth undone
    Say again   cloth whole"

Word from his mouth   cloth undone
Again his word   cloth formed

When gods   his fathers   see his word
                   rejoice
                   say homage:

{ "MARDUK   King!"
{ Sunchild

They give him then   scepter throne and ball
             invincible weapons   foe undoers

"Go!   Cut the breath of { TIAMAT
                          { Saltsea!
  The winds carry her blood to unknown lands!"

The gods   his fathers   setting fate for { BEL
                                 { Lord
            clear him way   { (MARDUK)
                     to full success

He makes a bow   calls it his weapon
   attaches the arrow
   fixes its cord

   picks a toothed-sickle   (holds it in his right hand)

   hangs the bow and quiver by his side

   sets it lightning in his face
   fills his body aflame

   makes a net   to catch { TIAMAT
                        { Saltsea

   sets the fourwinds to hold her all
       the Southwind
       the Northwind
       the Eastwind
       the Westwind
   puts the net
         { ANU
         { Sky   his father   gave
                          by his side

   makes:
       the Evilwind   Imḫullu
       the Stormwind
       the dust storm

                 the fourwind
                 the sevenwind
                 the wreckingwind
                 the peerlesswind

The winds he makes   he looses all 7
to stir ⌠TIAMAT
       ⌡Saltsea's guts   they rush at his back
The ⌠bel
    ⌡(MARDUK)   then raises   the Hurricane
                                              his great arm
                       mounts   his storm car
                                           peerless   terrible
                       yokes   a fouryoke   up
                                the Destroyer
                                the Ruthless
                                the Crusher
                                the Quick
                                       sharp toothed
                                       poisonous
                                       destruction familiar
                                       wrecking learned

Smiter   feared in battle   on his right
Combat   turns back the earnest   on his left
   clad   armorclad   in terror clad
horrible splendor covers his head

and the ⌠bel   went fast
        ⌡lord   along his way

and to ⌠TIAMAT   in her anger
       ⌡Saltsea   set his face
                               holds in his lips a spell
                               in his hands a plant against poison

This then his fathers race 'round him
         the gods   race 'round him
The gods   his fathers race 'round him
         the gods   race 'round him

The bel   comes up
    lord   sees in side ⎰TIAMAT
                           ⎱Saltsea   the forces of ⎰KINGU
                                               ⎱land
                                             her lover
               sees them   his way upset
                           mind confused
                           acts chaotic

The gods   his aids   march at his side
                       see the brave   the foremost
                       lose sight

⎰TIAMAT
⎱Saltsea   casts up her word   turns not her neck
  savage   lips   rebellion:

"How honored you are   ⎰BEL
                        ⎱Lord   of the gods
  They come with you
      leave their place
      come to yours"

The ⎰bel
    ⎱lord   rears the Hurricane   his mighty arm
to ⎰TIAMAT
   ⎱Saltsea   enraged   raises his word:

"So   you are supreme   superb
            make your own heart make war
                             sons hate fathers
        you spurn motherlove
        make ⎰KINGU
            ⎱land   lover
        make him   ⎰ ANU
                   ⎱ Sky   He is not
        plot ill for ⎰ANŠAR
                  ⎱Skyline   godking
        set evil against the gods   my fathers

Let your men stand in arms!
You be armed
Come on!   You meet me in duel!"

⎧TIAMAT
⎨Saltsea   hears these words
⎩   goes berserk
                  loses sense
                  cries madly   in piercing voice
                                          legs tremble both   full length
                  calls a spell
                  throws a curse

              Gods at war   sharpen arms

Come together ⎧TIAMAT and ⎧MARDUK
                      ⎨Saltsea   ⎨Sunchild   wisest wise
raise at each other
join for battle

The ⎧bel
     ⎨lord   casts his net
              catches her
              looses Imḫullu   in her face   from behind him

⎧TIAMAT
⎨Saltsea   opens her mouth   gobble him
He   sends in Imḫullu   she'll never close her lips

The furywinds puff her belly to heartache
                              her mouth gapes
He flies the arrow   it rips her belly
                            tears her gut
                            splits her heart

He binds her
    cuts her breath
    throws her body down
    stands up   on her

{TIAMAT
{Saltsea   killed   who marched first
Her troops scatter
    gang breaks up
    the gods her aids who marched alongside her
                          shake fear
                      turn backs to keep
                              save
                                their lives

Circled   they cannot run
{MARDUK   binds them
{Sunchild   breaks their weapons

Thrown in nets   ensnared
          in caves   wailing
His punishment they carry imprisoned   fettered

The Eleven   {TIAMAT
              {Saltsea   puffed full of horror
the Demontroop   marched at her face
he threw   in chains bound
their enmity   he crushed underfoot

{KINGU
{land   who was most strong
he bound   gave to {UGGU
                  {deathgod
    took off the Tablets of Fate
                      not *his* by right

                      sealed them with his seal
                      hung them on his chest

When he'd bound his enemy
        beat him
        dragged down the haughty foe
        completed the triumph of {ANŠAR
                             {Skyline

When ⎰MARDUK
    ⎱Sunchild   had done   the will of ⎧NUDIMMUD
                                      ⎨Manmaker
                                      ⎩(EA)
              made sure the captured gods
              turned again to beaten ⎰TIAMAT
                                      ⎱Saltsea
              stood her on her legs
              split her head
              cut her vessels
The Northwind   took off her blood   to Nowheres

His fathers see
          rejoice
          shout joy
          bring *him* gifts   homage

The ⎰bel
    ⎱lord   paused
           looked on her corpse

           splits the monster

           makes a fine thing:

           cleaves her like a clam
           puts up half for skies
           bars it separate   sets guards
                  to keep her waters

           Made way through heavens   looking there
             to make an Apsu   a dwelling for ⎧NUDIMMUD
                                          ⎨Manmaker
                                          ⎩(EA)

```
        measured it
      set up a house after it
        the ⌈EŠARRA
            ⌊Worldhouse
      the greathouse
          ⌈EŠARRA
          ⌊Worldhouse      he made the sky
                          made at home:
                                    ⌈ANU
                                    ⌊Sky

                                    ⌈ENLIL
                                    ⌊Earthgod

                                    ⌈EA
                                    ⌊Waterhome
```

---

*COLOPHON TO TABLET IV   . . . 146 lines   Tablet
IV of enuma eliš incomplete   after a damaged tablet
written by Nabu-bel-su   son of Na'id-Marduk the smith
for his soul's life   for his house's life   he wrote it   put it
in the Ezida*

```
He made stands for the great gods
    set the stars    like them   in lumasu-constellations
    set the year    limited
            for every 12 months   3 stars
    marked the year marks
    made the stand of ⌈NEBIRU
                      ⌊Crosser    to mark their limits
        that none may cross or err
    beside it set ⌈ENLIL       ⌈EA
                  ⌊Earthgod     ⌊Waterhome
            opened ports on either side
            fixed the left lock    and the right
```

In her belly set the height of heaven
     made ⌠NANNARU
        ⌡Newmoon   shine
    gave him night

    gave it the   night spangle
                    to make the days:
"Turn all   all months   the first
             unstopping
                your crown
shine hours   show 6 days
            the seventh day   a half crown
        half moons   two halves equal

When join ⌠ŠAMŠU
       ⌡the Sun   at Earthsky
                  bleach bit by bit
                  go back
         at the darkness   approach the ⌠ŠAMŠU
                            ⌡Sun   way
             again in opposition

Here see your sign   go its way
Come close to ⌠ŠAMŠU
       ⌡Sun   both rule
               no favor

      . . . .

He gave days to ⌠ŠAMŠU
          ⌡Sun
  set day and night bounds . . .

      . . . .

gathered ⌠TIAMAT
      ⌡Saltsea's   foamspit
made
melded clouds   full water
             raise wind
             make coolrain

made wet spit steam   piles
he did
    his hand

piled a mountain   her head
opened spring   rushing river
loosed   through her eyes { Parata
                           curvewater
                           (Euphrates)

                           { Idikla
                           current
                           (Tigris)

stopped her nostrils   held back water

piled mountains   her teats
dug sprays   channels

bent her tail up   bound to band
{ APSU
 Deepwater   underfoot
      her crotch   forks sky up

now: sky   top
    earth   set

made the womb   of { TIAMAT
                    Saltsea   run
pulled out his net
sky earth   limits set

Made his   godwork   done his god task
    made chapels   gave to { EA
                         Waterhome

    took   from { KINGU
                    land   Tablets of Fate

brought
gave   firstgift   gave ⎰ANU
                                ⎱Sky
                        gods of broken weapons
                                flight

shoved   bound   'fore fathers

⎰TIAMAT—built   eleven devils
⎱Saltsea   broken weapons   foot-irons

made likenesses   at Apsugate

"Here's a sign they won't forget!"

Gods   saw him there
         shone
         delighted
                 LAḪMU and LAḪAMU   all his fathers
⎰ANŠAR
⎱Skyline   came to him
          greeted him "King!"

⎰ANU ⎰ENLIL   ⎰EA
⎱Sky ⎱Earthgod ⎱Waterhome   give him gifts
⎰DAMKINNA   his mother   joys him with a gift
⎱Earthandskylady   shines his face with tribute sent

USMU   who brought her gift to hiddenplace
     he made Apsuwarden   chapelkeeper

⎰IGIGI   gathered
⎱heavenly gods   all bowed down

⎰ANUNNAKI   all many
⎱sky and earthgods   kissed his feet

All   all   came honoring
     before him   bowing:
"This is the King"

. . . .

In kingly aura   lifts the sickle
                    holds it right hand

                    slings the bow
                    takes the scepter
                          left hand

            . . .   his net   all glows the Apsu

            He sits
                    on his throneseat   in the chair

The gods   the many {EA   {DAMKINNA
                      Waterhome Earthandskylady

                  open mouth
                  say to great gods {IGIGI
                                    heavenly gods:

"Before {MARDUK
          Sunchild   our son
now   your king

Proclaim his name!"

They say together:
                      {"LUGALDIMMERANKIA
                       Kingofthegodsofskyandearth   his name

                    Trust him only!"

When reign to {MARDUK
                Sunchild   given
                      gave him plan   peace and well-being:

"From now   you keep the homes

  You word   we obey"

{ MARDUK   opens mouth
{ Sunchild   speaks
                      to gods
                        his fathers

         says:
"Above the Apsu   you live
like { EŠARRA
     { Worldhouse   I build for you
below the dirt I gather to build
I build a house   my pleasant home
inside   holy grounds
I raise   holy cells
  fix my reign

When you rise from Apsu for Assembly
      night's rest for all of you

When you come down from skies for Assembly
      night's rest for all of you

I name it { 'BAB-IL CITY
       { City at the Gods-gate

      homes of   the great gods'

I build it with craftmasters"

The gods   his fathers   heard his speech
                  asked { MARDUK
                      { Sunchild   firstborn
                          how this would be:

"On all your hands build
          who will have your agency?
Over the dirt your hands build
        who will hold your court?

In { BAB-IL   called in fortune
  { Godsgate   found our shrines   forever!

Let the rebel gods   serve us daily
       your agency   ours
       none else do our jobs"

. . . .

{ MARDUK   joyed
{ Sunchild   answered these gods

{ TIAMAT
{ Saltsea—killer
         opened mouth   nobly:

"I command them serve daily
         my agency in your hands"

Gods bow before him
     proclaim him
     say   to { LUGALDIMMERANKIA
         { Kingofthegodsofskyandearth:

"Before { BEL
       { Lord   was son
 Now   he is   our king
                whose bright words is our life
        Lord of splendor   sickle   scepter
                          all-skilled

Let { EA
    { Waterhome   plan
          We are the builders"

COLOPHON TO TABLET V   *Fifth tablet of enuma*
eliš   Palace of Assurbanipal   *king of the universe*
king of Assur

{ MARDUK   hears the oath of the gods
{ Sunchild   decides to build a fine work

              opens his mouth to { EA
                           { Waterhome
        tells   heart plan:

"I will heap up blood
      make a bone mass
      build up a humanbeing
      call it amelu
          man
 I will make humanbeing   amelu
                     man
 He will serve the gods
                   they will be eased
 So I will finish godways
                the same revered
                          in two groups"

{ EA
{ Waterhome   says to him these words
                        to ease the gods
        tells this plan:

"Only one of their brothers   cut loose
                  put alone to death
                      to make mankind
 Let the great gods Assemble here
 Cut loose the guilty   they will live"

{ MARDUK   Assembles   the great gods
{ Sunchild   directs   nobly
        gives orders

The gods   in place   hear him out
The Prince   says these words to the { ANUNNAKI
                             { sky and earthgods

"If you said truth before   swear now:

Who brought rebellion?
    made ⎰TIAMAT fight ?
         ⎱Saltsea
    led   the battle?

Turn him in that made rebellion

I'll bear him nemesis
    leave you in peace"

The ⎰IGIGI
    ⎱heavenly gods   great gods   say to him
                                    him
                        ⎰LUGALDIMMERANKIA
                        ⎱Kingofthegodsofskyandearth
                        godspeaker
                        their ⎰Bel
                              ⎱lord:
"It's ⎰KINGU   brought rebellion
      ⎱land   made ⎰TIAMAT
                        ⎱Saltsea   fight
                   led the battle"

They tied him
    brought face ⎰EA
                 ⎱Waterhome
    laid on him his guilt
    cut his blood

⎰EA   makes humankind   from his blood
⎨Waterhome   sets them   godservice
⎩(NUDIMMUD)   sets gods free

a work   that work   unknowable

                        crafty planned by ⎰MARDUK
                                          ⎱Sunchild

done by {NUDIMMUD / Manmaker}

{MARDUK / Sunchild}   king of gods   split the {ANUNNAKI / sky and earthgods}

        all of them   above   and below

    gave them to {ANU / Sky}   to see to his command:

    5×60 in sky   gods to guard there

    made   in the same way   the ways of earth

    in sky and on earth put 600 gods

After {MARDUK / Sunchild}   king   made law for all the gods
    set the laws for the {ANUNNAKI / sky and earthgods}
        of the sky and earth
    the {ANUNNAKI / sky and earthgods}   open their mouths
    say to {MARDUK / Sunchild}   their lord:

    "Now {bel / lord}   who sets us free
        what can we do for you?
    We build shrinchome   then   call it: see
    'Room-to-rest-nights'   may we sleep there"

When {MARDUK / Sunchild}   heard their words
    his face gleamed bright like the day:
    "Like another {BAB-IL / Godsgate}   built as you want
        bricks be made
        call it:

        {'PARAKKA' / Chapel}"

The {ANUNNAKI
{sky and earthgods use tools
                    one year long   make bricks

        second year comes and they raise {ESAGILA   head   high
                                          {Headraising   as Apsu deep

                build a ziggurat   high as Apsu
                            pinnacle
                make a house   a rest   for:

                    {MARDUK   {ENLIL   {EA
                    {Sunchild {Earthgod   {Waterhome

In glory he sat before them
            looked up from the bottom to {ESAGILA   horns   top
                                         {Headraising

When they had made the work of {ESAGILA
                               {Headraising
                                    the {ANUNNAKI
                                        {sky and earthgods
            made their own chambers

            gathered   all   at the {ESAGILA
                                      {Headraising
                    they had built for his rest

He set the gods   his fathers   down to feast:
        "This is {BAB-IL   your home
                 {Godsgate   which you love

            Come be happy in this place
                    make feast"

The great gods take their places
                    sit to drink zarbabu
                            festal beer
                    sit down to feast

                are happy inside
                        make rites in glorious {ESAGILA
                                               {Headraising

             then
                        fix laws and fates
                          posts in heaven and on earth
                            for all the gods

The fifty great gods sit
the seven gods of fate

                        make fate:

⎧ENLIL
⎨Earthgod   lifts   his bow   his weapon   (which he made)
⎩   puts it in front of them

The gods   his fathers   see the net   he made
                                see   the bow   its crafty make
                    his fathers praise the work he made

⎧ANU
⎨Sky   lifts it
⎩   praises it in the Godassembly

         kisses the bow: "This is my daughter"
         names the bow names:

                    Longwood first
                    . . . .   second
                    Star/bow   third   I make it shine in sky

Praise revenging son
over all   no equal
guard the black-headed   his makings
            mankind

                              who worship him forever
                              praise his ways
                              unforgetting

Let him make great foodgifts for his fathers

                              "ENUMA ELIŠ"   223

They keep the houses   support the offerings
     bring incense to be smelled   whisper prayer

       image on earth   what he makes in sky

Order the black-headed to worship
       subjects   remember their god
       obey the goddess   at his saying
       bring foodgifts for god and goddess
       support their gods   unfailing

       build up their lands
       build more shrines
       black-headed wait on their gods

For us he is god   by many names
We count his fifty names:

Whose acts are very splendid whose ways are splendid—
          ⌠MARDUK
          ⌡Sunchild
  ⌠ANU
  ⌡Sky his father called him coming out
Who sets food and drink   full stables
Who whips the enemy with his weapon abubu
                    Deluge
Who saved the gods his fathers in their trouble

Yes   truly   the Sun's child brightest god
May the gods always walk in the bright shining of his light

Who put godservice on the peoples he made
                    quickened
                       so we may rest

Making   wrecking   saving: his command
They will pray to him

{MARUKKA
(MARDUK)
God who makes everything
Makes the {ANUNNAKI
sky and earthgods   happy-hearted
                                        eases them

{MARUTUKKU
(MARDUK)
Truly   saves the land
        keeps the people

    the people praise him

{BARŠAKUŠU   ŠUTUNŠAKUŠE
                Thronekeep
Who lifts himself to rule the world
                greathearted   warmbreasted

{LUGALDIMMERANKIA
Kingofthegodsofskyandearth
the name we called him in Godassembly
raising his mouth's word over the gods his fathers
Truly {bel
lord of all the gods of earth and sky
        whose order subdues the gods

{NARI-LUGALDIMMERANKIA
President-Kingofthegodsofskyandearth
the name we have given him : Watcher of all the gods
Who in sky and on earth makes our seats safe   in trouble
        sets posts for the {IGIGI   and {ANUNNAKI
                earthgods   skygods
His name makes the gods shake   shiver in their seats

{ ASARULUDU
{ Judge
the name his father { ANU   named him
{ Sky
Truly   light of the gods   strong chief
who   like the { šedu and lamassu
{ protector genies
protects the gods and land
who saved our homes in trouble   in raging duel

{ ASARULUDU called too { NAMTILLAKU
{ Judge   { God of life
by all the 600 gods
Who rebuilds the lost gods   as his own creatures
The { bel
{ lord   whose pure spell rebreathes the dead gods
Foe beater   Praise him

{ ASARULUDU   third called { NAMRU
{ Judge   { Oath
The Pure God Who Shines Our Way

{ ANŠAR   LAḪMU   LAḪAMU   each called him three names
{ Skyline

said them to the gods   their sons

"Each of us called three of his names.
You call his names like us"

They rejoice   hear their word
in the { UPŠUKINNA   fix decision:
{ Fates' hall

"We will raise his name
brave son   revenger   protector"
and take their places in Godassembly to say fates
all together in holy place   fix his name

COLOPHON TO TABLET VI   *Sixth tablet of enuma*
eliš . . .

{ASARU
 Ruler
gives fertile fields   sets seeds
makes grain   herbs   sprouts the green

{ASARUALIM
 Heavy Ruler
honored in council house   first in counsel
the gods wait to him   when fearing

{ASARUALIMNUNNA
 High and Heavy Ruler
honored   light of his father   who fathered him
Who leads well commands of {ANU   {ENLIL   {EA
                                  {Sky   {Earthgod   {Waterhome

      their provider   fixes them income
whose šukussu-field is abundant   swelling

{TUTU
 Starter
who restarts them
Make the shrines pure   for rest
Make the spell   gods   rest
If they get up angry   they go back

Truly   first in the Godassembly
none of them his equal

{TUTU-ZIUKKINA
 Starter- Godband Life
Life of the Band of Gods
Who made the bright heavens for the gods
    holds their ways together
    sets their courses

May he never be forgotten among the hordes
his works be remembered

{TUTU third called {ZIKU
{Starter   {Purelife
Pure Maker
Sweet breaths' god
{bel
{lord   hearing and giving
makes richness and plenty
assures   the teem
makes our lack   fullness
whose sweet breath we breathe   in distress
Proclaim   Uplift   Worship his fame

{TUTU fourth called {AGAKU
{Starter   {Purecrown
the people praise him
{bel
{lord of pure spell   rebreathes the dead
                        pities bound gods
                        lifts the gods' levied yoke
                        makes mankind to save them work
Making mercy   whose power is to breathe life

His words last   unforgotten
in black-headed mouths   his hands' making

{TUTU fifth called {TUKU
{Starter   {Pure Spellspeaker
their mouth speak his pure spell
whose pure spell undoes the evildoers

{ŠAZU
{Heartknower
knows the hearts of gods
sees their guts
The evildoer cannot escape him
who sets Godassembly   makes their hearts happy
bends the rebel   shades the gods
wipes out evil   saves the right
keeps wrong   and   right apart

{ ŠAZU   second named { ZISI
{ Heartknower   { Lowlifter
quiets the rebel
        praise him
Takes away pain from the body of the gods   his fathers

{ ŠAZU   third named { SUḪRIM
{ Heartknower   { Foeloser
with arm   tears out the enemy
confuses their plots
winnows them in wind
erases the evil ones   shaking

Gods   praise him

{ ŠAZU called fourth { SUḪGURIM
{ Heartknower   { Foestamper
who sets court
    creates the gods   his fathers
destroys the enemy   smashes their children
confuses them
none left
Call his name
Say it everywhere

{ ŠAZU   called fifth { ZAḪRIM
{ Heartknower   { Foeruin
praise
destroys the enemy
hunts down evil
brought hunted gods home
His name go on forever

{ ŠAZU   sixth { ZAḪGURIM
{ Heartknower { Allfoeruin
give him all praise
destroys all the enemy in war

> { ENBILULU
>   { Adad of Bab-il

He is the grower god
                    strong
who names them
sets roastgifts
makes pasture and waterhole sure in the land
opens wells   sets waters

> { ENBILULU   second { EPADUN
>   { Adad of Bab-il   { Watercourser

praise him
who waters earth
washes sky and earth
sets planting
fixes land
            to plow
            to pasture

            dam and trench
            and furrow

> { ENBILULU   third { ENBILULU-GUGAL
>   { Adad of Bab-il   { . . . -Greatness

washes gods' crops
praise him
bel
lord of plenty
      of richness
      of heavy crops
gives richness
makes the homes rich
gives millet
drives up barley

<pre>
        ⎰ENBILULU   ⎰ḪEGAL
        ⎱Adad of Bab-il⎱Plenty
piles up plenty for the people
rains rich over wide earth
fixes green
</pre>

SIR.SIR

<pre>
piled up a hill on ⎰TIAMAT
                   ⎱Saltsea
carved ⎰TIAMAT
       ⎱Saltsea   with his weapon
guides the land   steady shepherd
his head:
           a field of grain
           field rows high
leaps the broad deep   in anger
crosses   a bridge walk   to duel
</pre>

SIR.SIR   second   MALAḪ

<pre>
his boat is ⎰TIAMAT
            ⎱Saltsea
                 he rides her
</pre>

GIL . . .

keeps grain heaps   huge piles
pushes up barley   millet
gives the land seed

GILMA

makes high godhouse last
builds fastness

barrel hoop
goods giver

AGILMA

high
takes the wave crown
makes the clouds
makes the sky last

ZULUM

who gives out lands
gives sections   foodgifts

$$\begin{cases} \text{MUMMU} \\ \text{Speaker} \end{cases}$$

builds sky and earth
orderer
makes sky and earth pure

               or

ZULUMMAR

          of strength unequal among gods

GIŠNUMUNAB

maker of all people
maker of the parts of the world
who disappeared $\begin{cases} \text{TIAMAT 's gods} \\ \text{Saltsea} \end{cases}$
made men of them

$$\begin{cases} \text{LUGALABDUBUR} \\ \text{Fatherking deepleader} \end{cases}$$

wrecked what $\begin{cases} \text{TIAMAT} \\ \text{Saltsea plotted} \end{cases}$

caught her weapons
strong base   from top to bottom

$$\begin{cases} \text{PAPGALGUENNA} \\ \text{Firstgreat of all lords} \end{cases}$$

prime of all lords
power prime
highest of his brothergods
  of all gods

     {LUGALDURMAḪ
     {Highhouse King
gods' tie
bel
lord of the {DURMAḪ
     {Highhouse
first in godhouse
highest god

     ARANUNNA

counsels {EA
    {Waterhome
who makes the gods his fathers
whose high ways no god can equal

     {DUMUDUKU
     {Dukuson
the {DUKU doubles his pure home
  {(temple) Pure Home
the {LUGALDUKU
  {Dukumaster does not judge without him

     {LUGALLANNA
     {Skyhigh King
whose power among gods is highest
bel
lord {ANU
  {Sky strength
who {ANŠAR
  {Skyline called to greatness

{ LUGALUGGA
{ Deathking
took them off in battle depth
who has all knowing   wideseeing

{ IRKINGU
{ Kingudragger
who took off { KINGU
             { land   in battle depth
passes rule on all
makes kingship sure

{ KINMA
{ Guide
who leads all the gods
gives direction
gods shake fear at his name
        shake in storm

{ ESIZKUR
{ Prayerhouse
comes high in prayerhouse
gods set gifts before him
so he give them work
no making without him
maker of 4 black-headed
without him no god sets length of days

{ GIBIL
{ Reedfire
fire that makes the point sharp
makes crafty arms in { TIAMAT battle
                     { Saltsea
widewise
sureseeing
so deepheart
gods cannot see the bottom

$\left\{\begin{array}{l}\text{ADDU} \\ \text{Stormwind}\end{array}\right.$

his name   covers the sky
his wind blowing good over earth
then his speech blow clouds away
leave food for the people beneath

$\left\{\begin{array}{l}\text{AŠARU} \\ \text{Leader}\end{array}\right.$

who leads the gods of fate
he owns their fate

$\left\{\begin{array}{l}\text{NEBIRU} \\ \text{Crossing}\end{array}\right.$

point of heaven-earth crossing
who cross must cross him
$\left\{\begin{array}{l}\text{NEBIRU} \\ \text{Crossing star}\end{array}\right.$ bright in sky
controlling   spinning around him
"He halves $\left\{\begin{array}{l}\text{TIAMAT} \\ \text{Saltsea}\end{array}\right.$

            Call him $\left\{\begin{array}{l}\text{NEBIRU} \\ \text{Crossing}\end{array}\right.$ holds the middle

keeps the skies' starcourse
the gods are his sheep   he is their shepherd

$\left\{\begin{array}{l}\text{TIAMAT} \\ \text{Saltsea}\end{array}\right.$ master

cuts her life short and tight
as long as mankind lives   till days grow old
let her fade away   and ever keep away"

$\left\{\begin{array}{l}\text{BEL MATATI} \\ \text{Lord of Earth}\end{array}\right.$

Father $\left\{\begin{array}{l}\text{ENLIL} \\ \text{Earthgod}\end{array}\right.$ calls him

because he made the distances and the hard ground

{EA
{Waterhome's heart was high   hearing the {IGIGI
                                       {earth and sky gods
                                                 call his names

"Whose names his fathers raise   I call my name: {EA
                                              {Waterhome

He rules my rites
   does my order"

Calling him {"ḫanša"   the great gods call him whose names are fifty
          {fifty

Keep his names   the guide explain them
the converse of wise and knowing
the father pass them to his son
herders of cow and sheep open ear to them
be happy with {MARDUK   {ENLIL
            {Sunchild   {Earthgod   of gods
so the land abound   and he grow rich

(Marduk)   His word is set
            His order unchanging
            No god calls back the word of his mouth

            Where he looks his neck looks too
            No god dares his wrath
            Widewise
            Deephearted

. . .

COLOPHON TO TABLET VII . . .

---

236   ORIGINS

BEROSOS, FROM THE *BABYLONIAN HISTORY*

A Greek text by Berosos, c. third century B.C., taken from a
Babylonian source, c. 1200 B.C. Text: Jacoby, ed., *Die Fragmente der Griechischen Historiker,* Vol. 1. ". . ." is used to
separate fragments.

Berosos says in the first book of his *Babylonian History*
that he lived during the time of Alexander the Great

that he had consulted the public records of Babylon
which had been carefully preserved for 150 myriad years

that these records contain the history
                         of heaven, earth, and sea
of the first birth of everything
of the kings and their deeds

. . .

in the first year
Oan/Ea came
from the Persian Gulf
fish body
but under the fish head
man's head
fish tail
but underneath
man's feet
speaking like a man
destroying the mind

you can see him still
in the temple

picture/costume/priest?

he spent the day with the people
he ate no food
gave them letters learning skill
how to start a city
write laws
mark the land
sowing reaping
everything

ever since they've found
nothing else useful

sun goes down
Oan went back to the sea
but he'll be back tomorrow

he lives in the ocean at night

then others came
same place
read about them in the Book of the Kings

Oan left his word behind
he talked about how the world was born
the first birth
and how people can live together

. . .

(Oan's word)

shadow and water
many born and living there

marvelous their holding their self-born form

men two wings
or four and double-faced

one body two heads maybe
both sexes
a man a woman?
or goat-footed goat-horned
or horse-footed

horse behind
man in front
hippocentaur
Jušparik
Siren

born and lived
bulls men-headed
dogs four-bodied fish-tailed
horses dog-headed horse-bodied fish-tailed

all kinds
plus swimmers creepers snakers
plus many more
you'd be surprised

they kept borrowing from each other

pictures of them
in Baal's Temple
Babylon

they all lived inside a woman
. she was their mistress
Omorka/Um-ruk
in Chaldean Thalath/Tiamat
in Greek Thalatta (sea)
equaling in number Selené (Moon)

. . .

things were like that
when Baal-Marduk came rushing in
and cut the woman in half
the lower slice he made earth
the upper the sky . . .

Baal-Marduk cut off his head
the other gods mixed his blood with earth
and made figures/people
that's how we get minds
and share in gods' thoughts

. . .

Baal-Marduk
Greek Dios the light/Zeus
cut open the darkness (of the woman)
he sliced sky and earth apart
put everything where it belongs
(this the Greeks call cosmos)

everything that lived
that could not bear
the power of his light
checked out

. . .

Baal-Marduk
saw that the ground was lonely
that it did not live
he said to one of the gods
"cut off your head"
rubbed earth in the blood
made people and animals
who can bear his light air

. . .

Baal-Marduk
made the stars and the sun and the moon
and the five wandering stars

ABYDENOS, TWO FRAGMENTS
FROM THE *CHALDEAN HISTORY*

Fragments 1 and 4 from the Greek text by Abydenos, third century B.C., taken from sources in Mesopotamia, c. 1200 B.C. Text: Jacoby, ed., *Die Fragmente der Griechischen Historiker*, Vol. 1.

1.

first the sea: Tiamat

but Baal Marduk shrunk her up

built places for everyone from her
put a wall around Babylon
first city

when it was time
he left

4.

when Titan Adam swelled up out of the ground
huge and proud
better than the gods
he built a tower where Babylon is now

when it started to walk near the sun
[El's?] winds came and
blew it down

the wreck: Babylon
what we speak: Babble
though it had once been one

Kronos El and Titan war

confusion of what had once been clear

meropes
"clear speakers"

the Hebrews call confusion $\begin{cases} \text{"BABEL"} \\ \text{god's gate} \end{cases}$

THE DESCENT OF THE GODS

A Hittite text, c. 1400 B.C. Text: *Keilschrifturkunden aus Boghazkoi*, XXVIII, #4 and #5.

Gods   in the sky
          in the dark earth   listening:

           Naras
           Napsaras
           Minkis
           Amunkis

           Ammezadus

                the oldest gods

                these gods' fathers
                        mothers:

           Anu
           Antu
           Isara

           Ellila
           Ninlila
               now settled gods   strong.

In the sky Alalu was king
      then Anu   prime god   stood
        Alalu sat athrone
    and Anu   bowed
          put the cup to his hand

Alalu was king nine years long
Anu fought him in the ninth and beat him

Alalu fled in dark earth

Anu sat athrone in Alalu's place
Anu   athrone

Strong Kumarbi gave him food

                bowed
                        put the cup in his hand

In the sky Anu was king nine years long
Kumarbi fought him in the ninth

                                        Anu   like Alalu

Anu faced Kumarbi's eyes   but could not

        fled his hands
                        a bird   loose in heaven
Kumarbi chasing
        catching feet
            casting down Anu

            biting balls off
                gulping down
                            sticking into stomach

        laughing   happy guts

Anu   looking back   speaking to Kumarbi:

            "Happy guts!   How be happy?
            A mighty weight grows inside:

            I fuck you with Stormer

            I fuck you with Tigris

Can you bear it?

I fuck you with Tasmisu.

Three horrible godseed.

At last   Kumarbi
                smash your head on the rocks
                            on your own mountain"

A Hurrian-Hittite text, c. 1400–1200 B.C. The language is
Indo-European with a Semitic admixture. Text: Güterbock,
The Song of Ulikummi.

Who   whose mind is wisdom   taking in   Kumarbi gods' father
I sing

Kumarbi takes wise thoughts into his mind:
         he plans an evil day
         he plots against the Stormgod
         he plots a usurper
Kumarbi takes wise thoughts into his mind
         strings them like beads

When Kumarbi had taken wise thoughts into his mind   he got up
from his chair right away   took a stick in his hand
         put the winds for fast shoes beneath his feet
         left his city Urkis
         came into ikunta lulli   (Cold Pond?)

When Kumarbi came into ikunta lulli a rock lay there
         Her length   three two-hour marches
         her width   one two-hour march and a half

         His mind pricked up at her under

         he lay with the rock
         his man-ness poured into her
         He took her five times
         He took her ten times

    (A hiatus of about forty lines. Impaluri, vizier to Sea, brings
a message from Kumarbi)

"Kumarbi   says   'Kumarbi must always be   father of the gods' "

The Sea spoke to Impaluri   when he had heard his words:
"Impaluri   my vizier   hold your ear to my words
  the words I tell you   Go and tell these words   certainly
  to Kumarbi:

  Go now   and say to Kumarbi:
                    'Why do you come to my house   and leave
                    in anger?
                    Fear takes my house
                    fear takes the slaves

                    Cedar incense is broken for you
                    food already cooked for you
                    singers keep their lutes ready
                    for you   day and night

                    So   get up
                    come back to my house' "

Kumarbi did get up   Impaluri walked in front of him
Kumarbi left his house
Kumarbi made travel
Kumarbi went into the house of Sea

And Sea said:
                    "Set up a seat for Kumarbi to sit on
                    set a table for him
                    Bring him to eat and drink
                    bring him beer to drink"
The cooks brought things to eat
the cupbearers brought him sweet wine to drink

                    They drank one time
                    they drank two times
                    they drank three times
                    they drank four times
                    they drank five times
                    they drank six times
                    they drank seven times

            (More broken and lost lines)

. . . stone gave birth to stone . . .
The midwives brought out his birth
the goddesses of fate and the Mother-goddesses took the child
              put him on Kumarbi's knees
Kumarbi began to be happy about this son
          began to dandle him
          began to give him a best name
Kumarbi said to himself:

          "What name shall I set on him
            this son
            the goddesses of fate
            and the Mother-goddesses
            gave me?

          He leapt from her body like a blade

          let him go on
          and his name be Ulikummi

          He will go up to the skies to be king
          He will beat Kummiya the best town
          He will attack the Stormgod
                pound him like powder
                stomp him like an ant
                and break Tašmišu off like a reed
          He will toss all the gods down from the skies like birds
                break them like empty pots"

When Kumarbi had said these words   he said on to himself:
          "Who will I give him to   this child?
          Who will take him for a gift?
          Who will hide him
                keep him in the dark earth?
          So the Sungod in the sky will not see him
          or the Moongod
          So the Stormgod   strong king of Kummiya
                        will not see him
                        will not kill him
          So Ištar   queen of Nineve   the   woman
                        will not see him
                        will not break him off
                              like a reed?"

Kumarbi said these words to Impaluri:
>"Impaluri   hold your ear to my words
>>the words I tell you
>>take a stick in your hand
>>put the winds for fast shoes
>>beneath your feet
>>go to the Irširragods
>>say these words   strong
>>to the Irširragods:

>>'Come
>>>Kumarbi   gods'father calls you to gods'house
>>>. . .
>>Come right away'"

>>>>>"the Irširragods
>>>will take him   the child
>>>carry him in the dark earth
>>>They will not let the greatgods see him"

When Impaluri heard the words
>>>>he took his stick in his hand
>>>>>put the winds for fast shoes
>>>>>beneath his feet
>>>>Impaluri went
>>>>>came to the Irširragods

Impaluri said the words to the Irširragods:
>"Come
>>Kumarbi   gods'father calls you
>>You will not know why but hurry
>>>>Come"

When the Irširragods heard the words
>>>>they came right away
>>>>>got up   and came
>>>>>the whole way at once
>>>>>came to Kumarbi

Kumarbi said to the Irširragods:

"Take this child   for a gift   care for him
take him into the dark earth
Hurry   right away
Set him up like a blade
on Upelluri's right shoulder

He'll grow a yard a day
                    a rod a month
His stone growth will put out the eye"

When the Irširragods heard the words
          they took the child off Kumarbi's knees
the Irširragods lifted up the child
                    bound him to their chests like cloth
                    lifted him up fast
                    set him on Enlil's knees
     Enlil lifted his eyes
          saw the child before the god
          a body of slate

Enlil said to himself:
               "Who is this child
                              the goddesses of fate
                              the Mothergoddesses raise?
               who will see   the wars of the great gods
               This is an evil plan of only Kumarbi
               who sets up a usurper   of slate
               against the Stormgod he set up"

When Enlil finished speaking
                    they put the child on Upelluri's right shoulder
                    like a blade

The slate grew   strong waters made him grow
He grew a yard a day
          a rod a month
                    his stone growth put out the eye

When it came to the 15th day
                              the stone had grown high
He knelt in the sea   yet like a blade he stood out
                                        above the water
                              the stone stood
                                        tall like a pillar
                    The sea came up to his belt
                    like a girdle

              He was lifted up like a tower
                reached the temples
                and the gods' chambers in the sky

The Sungod looked down from the sky
              saw Ulikummi
Ulikummi saw the Sungod

The Sungod said to himself:
                "What strong god stands in the sea there
                  his body not like other gods'?"

The Sungod of the skies   his face changed
                              he went down to the sea
                              he put his hands to his head
                              then lowered them to his sides
                              gave up his own anger

When the Sungod of the skies saw the stone
he crossed the mountains for a second time that day
he left
    went to the Stormgod

Tašmišu said   seeing the Sungod coming:

                "Why is he coming
                              the Sungod of the skies
                              king of the earth?
                  Why he comes   it must be heavy
                  not to be dealt with lightly
                  The war must be strong
                  the struggle must be strong

              Upset in heaven   death and hunger for the earth"

The Stormgod said to Tašmišu:
> "Set up a seat for him to sit on
> set a table for him to eat on"

They spoke   the Sungod came to their house
They set up a seat for him to sit on
> but he did not sit

They set a table for him to eat on
> but he took nothing

They gave him   a cup
> but he did not drink

The Stormgod said to the Sungod:
> "Is the chamberlain bad
> who set up a chair
> you did not sit in?
> Is the steward bad
> who set a table
> you did not eat from?
> Is the cup-bearer bad
> who gave you a cup
> you did not drink from?"

(More lost material; the Sungod must have told what he saw, placating the Stormgod)

The Stormgod said to the Sungod of the skies:
> "Bread on the table will be good
> Eat now
> Wine in the cup will be good
> Drink now
> Eat and be full
> Drink and be full
> then arise and go up to the skies"

The Sungod heard these words and was happy in himself
> The bread on the table was good
> He ate
> The wine in the cup was good
> He drank
> Then the Sungod arose and went up to the skies

When the Sungod of the skies left
the Stormgod took wise thoughts into his mind
The Stormgod and Tašmišu clasped each other
                          left the temple   the chamber
His sister Ištar came from the skies   brave
          Ištar said to herself:

              "Where are the two brothers running?"
                          she set herself
                               stood up
                          in front of her two brothers

They clasped each other
     went up to Mount Ḫazzi

The king of Kummiya turned his face
                          set his eye on the horrible Slate
He stared at the horrible Slate
He was angry   then scared

The Stormgod sat down on the ground
his eyes spilled tears like streams
The Stormgod   eyes full of tears   said:

              "Who can bear it
                          the violence of this one?
                     Who can fight it?
                     Who can bear it
                          the fear of this one?"

Ištar said to the Stormgod:
                     "My brother
                     He knows nothing
                     but he is tentimes brave
                          . . .
     (About thirty lines missing. Ištar seems to suggest herself as a
       fit adversary)

                          "THE SONG OF ULIKUMMI"   253

Ištar sang   set out a rock from the sea
A huge wave came up from the sea
The huge wave said to Ištar:
                    "Who are you singing to?
                    Who do you fill your mouth with song for?

                    The man is deaf
                                    hears not
                    His eyes are blind
                                    he does not see
                    He is not merciful
                    Go away Ištar
                    Find your brother
                    while Slate is not brave yet
                    while his skull is not horrible yet"

When Ištar heard this
                    she put out her fire
                    threw away her harp and galgalturi
                                    and golden jewels

                    . . .
          (She tells the Stormgod; he instructs Tašmišu)

                    "Tell them to mix the fodder
                            bring perfumed oil
                            anoint the horns of Šerišu
                            plate the tail of Tella with gold
                    They must turn the axle and wheels
                              put strong braces inside
                    and on the outside   for cover   heavy stone

                    They must call out the thunder storms
                    Rains   winds   breaking rocks for 90 miles
                                    swamping rocks for 800 miles
                    They must call the rains   and the winds
                    They must bring the lightning
                                          sharp-flashing
                          out from the sleep-chamber
                    They must bring out the carts
                    Set them up now
                    then report to me"

When Tašmišu heard the words   he hurried   raced
                    brought Šerišu from pasture
                    brought Tella from Mount Imgarra

                    Hitched them on the front porch
                    brought perfumed oil
                    anointed the horns of Šerišu
                    plated the tail of Tella with gold
                    turned the axle and wheels
                    put strong braces inside
                    covered the outside heavy stone
                    and called out the thunder storms
                              rains and winds
                    which break rocks for 90 miles

            . . .

        (About thirty lines lost)

He took a stand to fight
He took up his weapons
He took the wagons
    brought the clouds from the skies

The Stormgod set his face at Slate
              stared at him:
                    His height . . .

        (About fifty missing lines. The preliminaries of the battle
            are staged; are indecisive)

The gods heard the call
          took their places in the wagons
Aštabi leapt into his cart like a . . .
        arranged the carts   (Aštabi=
Aštabi thundered   Zababu=
        in thunder went down to the sea   Ninurta)

. . .

Slate shook the skies
                flapped the skies like an empty cloth
Slate grew high
Slate was on the earth   reached 1900 miles
                           up into the skies
                           reached the temple
                           and the gods'house
He was 9000 miles tall
        9000 miles wide
He overtopped the gate of Kummiya like a . . .
Slate rose over Ḫebat and the temple
Ḫebat heard no news of the gods
      could not see the Stormgod or Šuwaliyatta with her eyes
                                      (Šuwaliyatta=
                                      Nergal)

Ḫebat said to Takiti:
                  "I can't hear the Stormgod's word
                  I hear no news of Šuwaliyatta
                  and all the gods
                  Has this slate man Ulikummi beaten
                  my husband
                  the heavy Stormgod?"

Ḫebat said again to Takiti:
                  "Hear me
                  Take a stick in your hand
                  Put the winds   fast shoes
                  beneath your feet

                  . . . go
                  Maybe the Slateman has killed him
                            killed my husband
                                the heavy
                                Stormgod
                  Report back to me"

        (About fifty lines broken and lost. Takiti fails)

When Tašmišu heard the Stormgod's words
he got up right away
    takes a stick in his hand
    puts the winds   fast shoes   beneath his feet
    went up to the high tower
    stood across from Ḫebat   said:

            "The Stormgod has told me to go to a low place
until he fills the years fixed for him"

When Ḫebat saw Tašmišu   she almost fell off the roof
She would have fallen by one step   but the women of the palace
    held her   stopped her from falling

When Tašmišu finished speaking   he went down from the tower
                            went back to the Stormgod
Tašmišu said to the Stormgod:

            "Where shall we sit down?
            On Mount Kandurna now?
            If we sit on Kandurna
            another will sit on Mount Lalapaduwa
            If we do not
            there will be no king   in the skies above"

Tašmišu said again to the Stormgod:
            "Come
                    Let us go to the Apsu   see Ea
                        ask for the fatetablets

                When we come to the gate of Ea's home
                    we bow by the outer door 5 times
                            by the inner door 5 times
                        15 times when we come before Ea
                Maybe Ea will hear us
                            have mercy on us
                                give us back our reign"

The Stormgod hurried when he heard Tašmišu's words
            got up from his seat right away
The Stormgod and Tašmišu clasped each other
                    went the whole way at once
                    came to Apsu

                    "THE SONG OF ULIKUMMI"   257

The Stormgod came to Ea's house
        bowed 5 times by Ea's outer door
        bowed 5 times by Ea's inner door
When they came before Ea
     he bowed 15 times

             (Great fragmentation and loss. The Stormgod
             and Tašmišu enlist the aid of Ea)

Ea said to Enlil:
       "Don't you know Enlil?
       Has no word come to you?
       Don't you know him:
             the usurper Kumarbi shaped
                 against the Stormgod
             the Slate-man who grew up
                 in the water
             9000 miles tall
                 like a tower raised?"

        (More lost lines. Ea goes on to Upelluri)

When Ea finished what he had to say
he went to Upelluri

Upelluri raised his eyes
            saw Ea
Upelluri said to Ea:
       "Long live Ea"   and stood
Ea prayed life to Upelluri
        "Long live Upelluri on the dark earth
        the skies and earth rest on him"

Ea said to Upelluri:
       "Don't you know Upelluri?
       Has no word come to you?
       Don't you know him:
             the usurper Kumarbi shaped
                 against the Stormgod
             the Slate-man who grew up
                 in the water
             9000 miles tall
                 like a tower raised?

He has swamped the skies
                    the temples
                    Ḫebat
        Are you so far away from the dark earth
        Upelluri
        you don't know this hard god?"

Upelluri said to Ea:
        "When they built the skies and the earth on top of me
                I was not aware
        And when they came and cut the skies from the earth
          with a slicer
                Again I was not aware
        Now my right shoulder something hurts
                but I don't know who the god is"

Ea heard the words
    turned Upelluri's right shoulder
            The Slate-man stood
                    on Upelluri's right shoulder
                    like a blade

Ea said to the Old gods:
            "Hear my words   Old gods
            who know the old words

            Open the storehouses of old
            of father time   of grandfather

            Bring the seal   old   of fathers
            then seal again

            Bring out the first slicer
            which cut skies from earth

            This Slate-man   Ulikummi
            Kumarbi brought up as a usurper
            against the gods
            we will cut beneath his feet"

Tašmišu   on his knees   to Ea
          said:
    "He has changed . . .
    I see the dead
    all over the dark earth
    They are dust fallen
    the evil stands"

Ea said to Tašmišu:
    "I have already hit the Slate-man
    Ulikummi
    Now   go   and you fight him   second

    The Slate-man stands like a blade
        no more"

Tašmišu was happy
    called 3 times
    called into the skies

    The gods heard

    called 2 times

    The Stormgod   strong king of Kummiya heard

They came to Assembly
    all the gods
        roared bull-roars
            against
            the Slate-man
            Ulikummi

The Stormgod vaulted into his wagon like a . . .
    went down to the sea in thunder
    gave battle to the Slate-man   the Stormgod

The Slate-man said to the Stormgod:
    "I tell you what   Stormgod
    you beat against yourself

I tell you what   Stormgod
        you only beat against yourself
Kumarbi has a plan
        like beads on a string   in his mind
I will go up into the skies
        to be king
I will beat Kummiya   the best town
              the temple
              the chamber
and toss the gods down from the skies
              like birds

                    . . .

(The rest is lost. Kumarbi-Ulikummi must have lost)

A Hittite (Anatolian) text, c. 1350 B.C., under Mesopotamian influence; a text for recital during the Purulli (New Year) Festival. Text: Laroche, *Textes mythologiques hittites en transcription*.

The words for Kella, priest of the Stormgod of Nerik. The cultus tale for the Purulli Festival of the Stormgod of the Skies; no longer in use:

The land be fruitful and abundant. The land be guarded; so when it is fruitful and abundant, keep the Purulli Festival.

The Stormgod $\begin{cases} \text{IM} \\ \end{cases}$ (Tešub) and Illuyanka the Dragon fight in Kiškilušša; the Dragon Illuyanka beats the Stormgod.
The Stormgod calls on all the gods:
"Come help me."
The goddess Inara makes a feast:

>She fixed up a lot of everything—

>>vats of wine
>>vats of marnuwan liquor
>>vats of walḫi liquor

>>full and many

then went to Zigarata.
She ran into Ḫupašiya, a man. Inara said,
"Look, Ḫupašiya, I want to do this and that. I want you to help me."
Ḫupašiya said to Inara, "O.K. If I can fuck you, I'll go along and do what you want."
So he fucked her.
Then Inara brought Ḫupašiya home and hid him.
Inara put on her best things and vamped the Dragon Illuyanka up from his hole: "Look. I'm having a feast. Come eat and drink."

The Dragon Illuyanka came up with his boys. They ate and drank.
They drank up all the vats, then were full. So they couldn't go
back down into their hole.
Ḫupašiya came and tied up the Dragon Illuyanka with a rope.
The Stormgod came and killed the Dragon Illuyanka.
The gods supported him.
Then Inara built herself a house on a cliff near Tarukka.
She settled Ḫupašiya in the house.
She said to him: "When I go away don't you look out
the window; you might see your wife and kids."
Twenty days passed and the man opened the window and saw his
wife and children. When Inara came home, he cried, "Let me go home!"
Inara said to Ḫupašiya, "You won't be opening any more windows!"
She killed him, fighting, and the Stormgod spread sahlu-weed on
the ruined house. The man died unhappy.
Inara came back to Kiškilušša, and gave her house to the king.
So the king owns Inara's house.

This is how the story was told later:

The Dragon Illuyanka beat the Stormgod, took heart and eyes from
him. The Stormgod wanted revenge.
He took a slave's daughter to be his wife. He fathered a son.
When the son grew up he married the daughter of the Dragon
Illuyanka.
The Stormgod tells his son:

> "When you go to your wife's house ask for heart and eyes."

When he got there he asked for heart and they gave it to him.
Then he asked for eyes and they gave him. He carried them back
to the Stormgod, his father. So the Stormgod got his eyes and heart
back.

When the Stormgod's body was back in shape, he went to the sea
to fight.

He fought the Dragon Illuyanka   and almost beat him. But the son
of the Stormgod, who was with Illuyanka, called into the skies
to his father:

"I'm with him.
Take me with him!"

So the Stormgod killed the Dragon Illuyanka and his son too,
and revenged himself on Illuyanka.

FROM HESIOD, *THEOGONY*
(ZEUS AND TYPHOON)

This Greek tale of Zeus and Typhoon is from Hurrian-Hittite
and earlier Indo-European traditions. The Greek text dates
from c. 600 B.C.; the Indo-European forerunners, from before
2300 B.C. Text: Hesiod's *Theogony* (West, ed.).

Zeus stuffing chalkmen Strainers into dead wombs underground Finish

Typhoon last son of monster Earth from father Pit the Death
                    through golden Love
            in his hands held strong acts
                    his feet of gods never hurting never rest
shoulders hunching a hundred heads each a dragon snake of fear
                    that flick dank dusky tongues
            his eyes gouting flame peeled look out
                    from god-mock heads
in each astounding face a voice a wordnoise no other god re-makes
                    stately Typhoon spoke
    god-tongue bull-bellow lion-waul shaking his unguarded heart
                    dog-whelp (that's hard to swallow)
whistle streaking through air that made mountains back his tunes
                    this day something might have happened
            no one could make up: Typhoon new king of gods and men
                    if old king Zeus
hadn't had sharp eyes slithery mind
                    cracked untired thunder so stiffly
            earth sky sideless sea Ocean rivers pit wombs below
                    echoed threw it back
when her king rose up in war his deathless feet shook Olympos
                    Earth wailed
            Zeus ranting his thunder lash
                    Typhoon screaming fire
flared into sunheat that checked the violet sea
                    they filled the wind then snapped it away
            turned earth sea sky to ceaseless restless
                    foam scum

soared up shake waves that combed foreshores headlands
inside and around
slapped Earth with timeless hands
so she couldn't stop heaving
ran fear into Hades unseen king of those who wait and rot
into the Strainers circling Kronos beneath Pitdeath
who hid from their cries that swept tides
from their fight with death in the other
Zeus hoisted his strength strapped on lightning thunder
sparkling flash
leapt from Olympos
struck
roared off
every godword head
from wonderful
Typhoon
who
lady-tamed
cut-whipped
by the bundled
voltage sticks
thrown
tumbled
head down
until he sprawled
a slag heap
on his mother's lap
monster Earth
cried
storm-broken
king Typhoon
flickered fire
in secret forests
on the jagged mountain
where he'd been sheared
flaring godword breath
he burned monster Earth
like the lead

                    smelters cook in groundpit holes
like iron strongest metal
                         fire lady-bends
                              in hill forests
          molten on goddess Earth
                         in palms of Hephaistos
                              his breath
                         roaring blaze
                                   softened
                         made her run
in his heart
               Zeus cried
                         threw Typhoon
          into father
                         broad Deathpit

Typhoon's children are the winds of strong water
                         except the North and South
               and West who clears off clouds
          gods bring these to help us before we die
no telling when typhoons will blow
                         random fitful flaws panting on the sea
               trouble when they fall on Ocean
                              when he is misty dark
their pitdeath breath scatters ships sinks sailors
                         helpless whoever they catch
               in flower time they rip up boundless Earth
                              murder the acts of love
people born to earth commit on her
                         stopping them
               with dust with difficult voice

FROM HESIOD, "THEOGONY" (ZEUS AND TYPHOON)   267

FROM APOLLODORUS, THE *LIBRARY*

(ZEUS AND TYPHON)

This Greek tale of Zeus and Typhon by Apollodorus, c. third
century B.C.–first century A.D., is drawn from a pre-Hesiodic
source in Greek, which in turn comes from earlier Indo-
European sources. Text: Apollodorus, *Bibliotheca* (Frazer,
ed.).

1.

                    the gods Old Thunderers destroyed
            the giants angry Earth
    in anger
                    fucked Tartarus
            did let him father Typhon on her
    cave-birth
                    between man & beast
            his size & strength were
    greater than Earth's other children
                    human to thighs bulked
            large above all
    mountains
                    whose head for largeness
            brushed the stars
    his hands reached east & west
                    projected
            a hundred dragons' heads
    down from the thighs snakes
                    coiled pulled erect
            to reach his head
    were hissing feathers
                    on his body
            wild hair flew out in
    wind from head
                    to cheeks 't was
            like fire in his eye

so tall
                        old Typhon was
              hurled burning rocks
was screeching
                        hissing
              spouted a jet of fire from
his mouth
                        en route to heaven

2.

                        careening toward sky was Typhon
              sighted by gods
escaped him
                        made for Egypt
              there they would change to
animals
                        one left behind
              Old Zeus Bright Sky
far off could volley
                        thunderbolts
              would close in flatten him with adamantine
sickle
                        there goes monster-
              man he's almost
in Syria 's got old Zeus
                        pursuing (sez)
              "he's wounded"
wrestles him now entangling
                        himself in Typhon's
              coils entwined
who grasps the sickle
                        severs the sinews of
              his hands & feet
& hoisted on shoulders
                        through the sea he hauls

                        the Thunderer back to
his cavern home
                                will drop him hide
                sinews in bearskin
sets a guard there
                                "Dragon Lady"
                "Dolphin"
"Virgin"
                                halfway created between
                man & beast

3.

                                in sequel
                Hermes Pillar God came
& Goat Pan
                                stole the sinews back
                made Zeus a perfect
fit (who saw it?)
                                        's got his strength again
                Zeus
in a chariot of winged
                                horses riding down sky hurled
                thunder at Typhon
chased that monster to
                                Lame Mountain
                where the Fates would trick him
got him to taste
                                "ephemera"
                are fruits they said would
strengthen him
                                from there to Thrace again
                pursued battled around
the bloody hill tossed up whole
                                mountains Zeus thrust
                back at him by force of
thunderbolt

                    a stream of blood
             gushed from
its rocks thereafter called
                    Blood Mountain

4.

                    in flight through
             the Sicilian Sea
old Zeus threw Aetna on him
                    "that great mountain"
             to this day erupts with
fire
                    thunderbolts
             touched off when thrown
ages before

FROM OPPIAN, *HALIEUTICA*

This Greek text by Oppian, c. third century A.D., stems from a pre-Hesiodic source in Greek, which in turn comes from earlier Indo-European sources. Text: Oppian, *Halieutica* (Mair, ed.).

                savior of Zeus but Typhon's
                              slayer
                     tricked the old snake-
           man with promises
                                   banquets of fish
                     (he said)
           would draw him from his
                              deep hole to the sea's
                     edge vulnerable
           to their lightnings
                              crack-of-fire
                     thunderbolts that flattened him
           blazed in that heat storm
                              beat his hundred heads on
                     rocks
           carded like wool the yellow
                              dunes still red with Typhon's
                     blood o Hermes
           counselor
                              god of fishermen
                     among old powers of
           the hunt

THE BATTLE BETWEEN YAM AND BAAL

A Ugaritic (Canaanite) text, c. 1450 B.C. The Ugarites were a Semitic people of the north Syrian coast. Text: Gordon, *Ugaritic Textbook*, Text 68.

KOTHAR WA-KHASIS   (Smart & Slick)
says:

> "Oh Prince BAAL   (Lord)
> I told you once
> I'll tell you again
> Rokhab 'arafot: (Cloud Rider)
>
> Your enemy Baal
>   Now
> Your enemy
>   Now
> Crush him!
>   Now
> Destroy your troubler!

You'll be king of the world   have your way forever"

Kothar lays out two clubs
   tells their names:

> "Your name
> you are
> YAGRUŠ   (Chaser)
>
> Chaser
> chase YAM   (Sea)

Chase Yam off his seat   NAHAR off his throne   (River)
Whirl in Baal's hand   an eagle between his fingers
Hammer Royal Yam
   Judge Nahar   in the back
       between his shoulders"

The club whirls   in Baal's hand
      an eagle   between his fingers
    hammers   the back of Royal Yam
                 between the shoulders
                 of Judge Nahar

Yam is not moved   his face is unchanged
      He is not pressed

Kothar lays out *two* clubs
    tells their names:

             "Your name
             you are
             AYAMUR   (Presser)

             Presser
             press Yam
      Press Yam from his seat   Nahar from his throne
      Whirl in Baal's hand   an eagle between his fingers
      Hammer Royal Yam
             Judge Nahar   on the head
                        between the eyes
          Yam will tumble   fall to the ground"

The club whirls   in Baal's hand
      an eagle   between his fingers
    hammers   the head of Royal Yam
                 between Judge Nahar's eyes

Yam tumbles   falls to the ground
His face falls   he is moved

Baal drags Yam   lays him out
    ready to finish off Judge Nahar

"Slow down"   Athtart calls
"Shame"   she cries to Aliyan Baal
"Shame"   to Cloud Rider

"Royal Yam   is our prisoner
  Judge Nahar is our prisoner"

Baal is shamed at the word of her mouth

THE BATTLE BETWEEN MOT AND BAAL

A Ugaritic tale. Text: Gordon, *Ugaritic Textbook*, Text 49 VI.

MOT laments: (Death?)

> "My brothers   my mother's sons
>   Baal makes
> my enemies   my killers"

He returns to Baal in the Northern Close
  lifts his voice
  shouts again:

> "My brothers   my mother's sons
>   Baal makes
> my enemies   my killers"

They circle at each other
        like stags

    Mot fierce
    Baal fierce

They gore each other
        like buffalo

    Mot fierce
    Baal fierce

They bite each other
        like snakes

    Mot fierce
    Baal fierce

They trample each other
        like running beasts

                    Mot fallen
                    Baal fallen

From on high ŠAPAŠ   (Sun)
cries to godson Mot:
                    "Hear me:

                    You set yourself
                    against Aliyan Baal?
                    How?

                    As Bull EL   (God)
                    your father
                    hears you
                    he will uproot
                    your house base
                    he will overturn
                    your kingly chair
                    he will break
                    your judgment stick"

Godson Mot   fears
El's dear brave   takes fright

                    . . .

        (Baal is made king)

THE BATTLE BETWEEN ANAT AND THE FORCES OF MOT

A Ugaritic tale of Anat's battle for her brother Baal. Text: Gordon, *Ugaritic Textbook,* 'nt II.

The Virgin Anat
Camouflages her divine aura
And puts on

The smell of goats and rabbits

She closes both the doors
Of the Palace of Anat

She catches up to the troops
In the mountain's slit

In the valley
Between the cities
How she slays them!:

She cleaves the Shore folk
She smashes the Western man.

All around her

Heads—a swarm of locusts
Hands—like crickets, as many
Soldiers' hands as thorns on cactus

Anat bundles up her
Prize

She loads up the heads
On her back:
She ties the hands
On her belt.

And, returning from
The valley

Her knees slosh through
The soldiers' blood,
The soldiers' flesh
Up to her hips.

She prods the captives
With the back of her bow.

And Anat comes home
Unsatisfied with her slaughters
In the valley.
She fights on, indoors.

                              She sets up

Chairs for soldiers
Tables for soldiers
Stools to be soldiers.

                         How she slays them!:

She smites them, then
Stands back
Her liver full of laughter
Her heart filled with joy
Overjoyed
For her knees wade in
Soldiers' blood:
Soldiers' flesh
Up to her hips.

When she has finished
Fighting in the house
Lunging between the tables

                              She is full

And she rubs her hands
In the soldiers' blood.

                         She pours the rich oil
                         Into a basin

And she washes
Her hands

Virgin Anat
Washes
Her fingers

The Sister-of-the-Peoples
Washes
Her hands in the blood
Of the soldiers
Her fingers in the gore
Of the soldiers

The chairs are only chairs again
The tables, tables
The footstools, footstools

                                        She pours out water

To wash
In the dew of the heavens
In the oil of the land
The rain from Cloudrider.

The Heavens' dew
Bathes her.

                                        The rain bathes her.

THE BATTLE BETWEEN ANAT AND MOT

A Ugaritic tale of Anat's battle in which she avenges her
brother Baal. Text: Gordon, *Ugaritic Textbook*, Text 49 II.

ANAT yearns for him   (Skylady?)
                    the heart of a cow for her calf
                    the heart of a ewe for her lamb
                    the heart of Anat for Baal

She catches Mot by a tear in his clothes
     grabs him by the edge of his sash
She raises her voice
     calls:

                    "You
                     Mot
                     Give back my brother!"

Godson Mot answers the Virgin Anat:
                    "What do you want from me?

               I was wandering
               Walking through all the mountains
                         into the very liver of the earth
                              through every hill
                         into the very liver of the land

               My breath   to man
                         was lost
               my breath   into the noise of earth

               I came to the pleasant land of Dabr
               to the beauty of the fields of Šiḫlememat

               I ran into Aliyan Baal

I put him in my mouth
                    like a lamb
                    like a kid
I chewed him up

The torch of the gods   Šapaš
glowed in the sky
                    at godson Mot's handiwork"

Day has passed after day
days have become months
Anat yearns for him
                    the heart of a cow for her calf
                    the heart of a ewe for her lamb

                    the heart of Anat for Baal

She catches godson Mot   slices him with a sword
                              tosses him in a sieve
                              scorches him in fire
                              grinds him with millstones
                              plants him in fields
                    so birds may eat him
                    sparrows eat his little bits
                    flitting from bit to bit

THE BUILDING OF BAAL'S PALACE

This Ugaritic text is included in this volume because Baal's palace is the earth in microcosm, as are temples. Text: Gordon, *Ugaritic Textbook*, Text 51 IV–VI.

(Athtart speaking):

> "He calls to Athtart   and her sons
>   to the goddess
>   and all her offspring
>
> 'Look
> there is no house for Baal
> as the gods have
>   no court
> as Athtart's sons have
>
> El's home is a shelter for his son
>
> the home of Lady Athtart of the sea
> is a home
>   for the untouched brides:
>   Pidraya's home
>   the daughter of light
>   Talaya's home
>   the daughter of rain
>   the home of Artsaya
>   the daughter of Y'bdr.'"

El   of the gentle heart says:

> "Am I to be an agent of Athtart
>   carrying hods?
>
> If Athtart will be a slave
>   making bricks
> a house will be built for Baal
>   as the other gods have
> a courtyard
>   fit for a son of Athtart"

Lady Athtart of the sea says:

> "Lord of the gods in wisdom
> your gray beard has taught you

> Now again Baal keeps rain season
> mud season
> gives his voice in the clouds
> lets lightning loose to earth

> He will make whole a house of cedar
> He will erect a house of bricks

> The word shall be taken to Aliyan Baal:

> 'Call the carpenter to your house
> the bricklayer inside your palace

> The mountains will crop you much silver
> the hills   beautiful gold
> the mines will crop you lapis

> So build a house of silver and gold
> a house of lapis jewels' "

Virgin Anat is happy   her feet thump the ground
She sets her face   at once   for Baal at Northheight
across a thousand fields   many many measures

Virgin Anat laughs
lifts her voice
shouts:

> "Be told   Baal   your telling   I bring you

> a house will be built for you
> like your brother's
> a court
> like your kin's

Call the carpenter to your house
the bricklayer inside your palace
The mountains will crop you much silver
the hills   beautiful gold

Build a house of silver and gold
a house of lapis jewels"

Aliyan Baal is happy
He calls the carpenter to his house
the bricklayer inside his palace
The mountains crop him much silver
the hills   beautiful gold
the mines crop him lapis

He sends for Kothar wa-Khasis

When Kothar wa-Khasis comes
he scts an ox in front of him

a fatling before his face
A seat is set
he sits   at Aliyan Baal's right
while they eat   and drink

Then Aliyan Baal says:

"A house in a hurry   Kothar
A palace rising fast

Build a house quickly
Raise a palace fast
in the middle of Northheight
The house will be on a thousand fields
the palace   many many measures

Kothar wa-Khasis says:

"Hear   Aliyan Baal
and consider   Cloudrider

I'll set a window in the house
a window in the side of the palace"

Aliyan Baal says:

> "Do not set a window in the house
>> a window in the side of the palace"

> (Because, apparently, Yam might use
>> the window to get at Baal's "brides")

Kothar wa-Khasis says:

> "Again Baal what I say
> once more   the word of Kothar wa-Khasis:

> 'Hear me   Aliyan Baal
> I'll set a window in the house
>> a window in the side
>> of the palace' "

Aliyan Baal says:

> "Do not set a window in the house
>> a window in the side
>> of the palace"

Kothar wa-Khasis says:

> "You will hear my word again   Baal"

His house is being built   palace raising

He goes to Lebanon for its trees
> to Siryon for its beautiful cedars

He sets fire in the house
> flames in the palace

So the first day and the second

>> fire eats in the house
>> flames   in the palace

> the third and fourth days

>> fire eats in the house
>> flames   in the palace

> the fifth and sixth days

>> fire eats in the house
>> flames   in the palace

Then on the seventh day

>> fire leaves the house
>> flames   the palace

Silver is made into tiles
Gold is made to bricks

Aliyan Baal is happy:

   "I built my house of silver
    my palace of gold"

Baal prepares his house
HADD   (Baal)
 prepares his palace:

    He slaughters cattle and sheep
     kills bulls and fatlings
       rams and calves of one year
       lambs and kids

    He calls his brothers into his house
       his kin inside his palace
    He calls the seventy sons of Athtart

    He fills
      the ramgods with wine
    He fills
      the ewe-goddesses with wine
    He fills
      the oxgods with wine
    He fills
      the cow-goddesses with wine
    He fills
      the thronegods with wine
    He fills
      the throne-goddesses with wine
    He fills
      the gods with jugs of wine
    He fills
      the goddesses with vats of wine

All the time the gods   eating and drinking
the breast-suckers making happy

a salted knife and a slice of fatling
drinking wine from a cup
treeblood from a golden cup

YHVH'S BATTLE WITH THE SERPENT

These Canaanite-Hebrew texts, c. 1500 B.C., are remnants of a Canaanite myth contained within the Hebrew Bible. Text: Kittel, *Biblia Hebraica*.

Is. 51:9–10

Waken
Waken
Gird might of arm
YHVH
Waken as before endless generatings

Didn't you crush Rahab?
        hole Tannin?
Didn't you dry up Yam?
        mighty waters of Tehom?
          set the ⎰YAM deeps a path for the saved to tread?
              ⎱sea

Job 26:12–13

In his might he stirred the ⎰sea
                      ⎱YAM
Then in his cunning crushed Rahab
By his wind set ⎰YAM in net
              ⎱sea
His hand made holes in the twisty snake

Ps. 74:13–17

You broke up ⎰YAM in your might
             ⎱sea
You smashed Tannin-heads in the water
You crushed Leviatan heads
Made him food for desert folk

You split spring and creek
You dried up   mighty rivers
The ⎰day is yours
     ⎱yom
The night is yours
You set up light and sun
You determined earthbounds
Summer and winter
                   you made them

           Ez. 29:3–6a

"See me
   I overcome you Pharaoh king of Egypt
            great Tannin squatting in the middle of its rivers
               saying: 'My Nile. I made it.'

I put hooks in your cheeks
   stick the fish of your Nile to your scales
I drag you up from the middle of your Nile
           with all the fish of your Nile stuck on your scales
I throw you out on the desert
        you and all the fish of your Nile

You fall upon the field
You will not be brought to burial
                 but I give you
to the earthlife and skybird for eating

So all the Egyptians may know that I am YHVH"

           Ez. 32:2–8

"The lion of nations you think yourself
   You are like Tannin in the sea:
        You tear up your rivers
        You churn the water with your feet
          muddy the rivers

This is what YHVH says:
'I spread my net upon you
                              and a group of many peoples
I drag you up in my snare
   throw you out on the land
   cast you on the field
   settle all the skybird on you
   stuff all the earthlife with you
   put your flesh on the hills
   fill the valleys with your carcass
   water earth with your flow
                              from your blood
   the channels will be full of you

I will extinguish you by covering the skies
                              darkening the stars
I will cover the sun in cloud
            the moon will not light its light
I will darken all the lights in the sky upon you
         and put darkness on your land'

The speech of Adonai YHVH"

THE PHOENICIAN ORPHIC THEOGONY
ACCORDING TO HIERONYMOS
AND HELLANIKOS

This Greek theogony, c. 500 B.C., is taken from a Phoenician source of c. 700–800 B.C. Text: Diels-Kranz, *Die Fragmente der Vorsokratiker*, Vol. 1.

Water and Lady Hyle

then she got tough: Earth

he cuts and scatters
she hugs and mingles

who came before them?
don't ask
you don't want to say the name

Water and Earth's child
"he-water-and-she-earth"
dragon snake
two heads bull and lion
in between a god (man) face
shouldering wings
called Chronos 'Olam the Timeless
and Heracles Mel-kart

to Chronos came Need
who is Nature
the Inevitable
without a body
stretching out her stick
to scratch in limits for everything

                    Chronos—Need
                    the man—woman
                maker of everything

the three children of dragon snake Chronos:
                knowing FireAir
                boundless Gap   set in the middle
                foggy NightPlace

    inside his three Chronos laid Egg
            or he made his three Egg

                    inside Egg
                    Male and Female
                        the seeds of everything

    and the third an unembodied god
                gold wings on his shoulders
            his ribs bulls' heads
                    a huge dragon snake wearing his head
        he can take the body of everything that lives

                    he is mind

                Egg father

        Male and Female power

who is the third of the third three?
                    First Born
                    Zeus Disposer
                    Pan All

EMPEDOCLES, FROM *NATURE*

Fragments from the Greek text by Empedocles, c. 500 B.C., which in turn was probably taken from a Near Eastern source, c. 800 B.C., via the Greek Orphics. Text: Empédocle: *Les Origines* (Bollack, ed.).

Origins

I speak in two

sometimes   one grows from many
sometimes   many splits from one

two   the birth of deathly life
two   the leaving off

birth   the union of all makes and kills
leaving off   strips and is stripped

when deathly life divides itself
exchanges never cease

sometimes   through Love everything grows into one
sometimes   through Hate everyone splits in two

when one splits once again
many are born but do not live forever

since this exchanging never ceases
they are always motionless in a circle

say it once
say it twice

I speak in twos

sometimes   one grows from many
sometimes   many splits from one

Fire and Water and Earth and the high unfilled measure of Air

Hate hated twice by the roots equals them
Love that's in them becomes their friend in length and width

mind, look at her
don't sit there eyes astounded

born in their bodies
men worship her

she makes them think of desire
doing what joins them in peace and friendship

so they call her JOYOUS JOINER
Gethosyné   Aphrodite

no one alive has ever seen her
because she swirls in their eyes

all the roots are equal
the same in birth and age

ruling with different honor
each according to their nature

time sails in a circle
each has a chance

nothing added to them
nothing taken away

always the same
equal in birth and age

if they should leave off without limit
everything would die

all this—what makes it grow?
where did it come from?

how should the roots leave off
since nothing is empty of them

always the same
equal in birth and age

running across each other
they make all things

so on so forth forever

I will tell you something else
everything that is born and dies
is not really born
does not really die
it only mingles and exchanges
what has already been
mingled and exchanged

people call this "birth"
I will use the same words
"birth" and "death"
since that is the custom

when Light and Air
mingle

to make the body of a man
or animal tree bird

people say "it has been born"

when men animals trees birds leave off
people say "it has died"

there is no birth
there is no death

only mingling exchanging
the already mingled and exchanged

birth and death
are names people use

I use them
because they do

but there is
no birth no death

you are a fool
if you think there is

this in the marvelous bending of the human body

sometimes   through Love
all the limbs unite
all the limbs that have a right to a body
at the peak of flowering life

sometimes   through Hate
all the limbs are dismembered
broken into pieces
by the Strifes smashers of life

this also happens to trees
fish who live under Water's roof
animals in the hills
even the tumbler pigeon
who walks on his wings

so on so forth forever

Love

clinging Love kisses

see the hot bright Sun everywhere

the immortals bathed in heat in thick light
the rain everywhere icy and black

from Earth
the gracious and solid
flow forth

coming together in Love
desiring each other

from all that was
all that is or
ever will be

trees leave

men and women and animals and birth and fish Water feeds
and the long-lived gods honored above all else

there is no death
their life is not forever

always the same
equal in birth and age

running through each other
making everything that is

the exchange the roots
mixing mingling bring

The Four Roots

the goddess says
"think of painters
they use the drugs of many colors
to make figures that look like real things
giving body to trees men women
to animals and birds
fish Water feeds
even the long-lived gods honored above all else

this is the origin of everything
that flowers without number by day"

the names of the four roots of everything

      ZEUS
      bright Air

      HERA
      mother Earth

      AIDONEUS
      homeless Fire

      NESTIS
      Water   who with her tears
                 waters life's well

time sails in a circle
each has a chance

losing itself in each other
growing according to their share

always the same
running across each other

born men and animals
trees birds fish

so on so forth forever

born hair leaf
thick bird feathers
horn scales on strong backs
tall tree perch in the sea

so on so forth forever

parts looking for bodies
heads without necks
suddenly sprouting in Earth like cabbages
naked arms shoulderless
eyes watching for sockets
monsters
roaming Earth
rolling feet shambling hands

born two faces two bodies
cattle man-prowed
men beeve-headed
half male half female
their bodies in shadow

sometimes   through Love the roots come together to make one
sometimes   through Hate the roots split to make many

grown into one
they are completely swallowed

knowing how to grow into one from many
to be many after one splits into two

this way they give birth
but their life is not forever

since they never cease mingling and exchanging
they are always motionless in a circle

Love	Harmony	Aphrodite
Hate	Strife	Neikos

when Strife reaches the bottom of the dyne
Love is born in the midst of the swirl
everything assembles there to be 'one and only'
not quickly
but one from one
one from another
deliberately
coming together
mingling and mixing
then the countless tribes of living things
flow forth

Strife holds up above
all who refuse mixing and mingling
alternating with those who do

for Strife has not yet retired perfectly
from the furthest rim of the circle
part of him remains
the rest escapes the body of Sphere

he retreats
soft Love's immortal attack pursues

suddenly the living are born to die
although they'd learned not to

when they mingle and exchange
the countless tribes of the living
flow forth
shaped to hold every body
wonderful to see

Air with his long roots enters Earth
Fire burns underground

A kiss unites everything in every part
radiant Sun   Earth   Sky   Sea

partly they live in the living
but their life is not forever

everything ripe for mixing mingling
Aphrodite matches
submitting to each other
they grow one

everything that is in two
split
in birth
in mixing and exchanging
in image set upon it
is enemy to itself
to everything else that is in two
they do not know how to join in Love
they are lonely sad
because Hate and Strife are twin fathers of their race

Sphere Cosmeg

Sphere rounded in Harmony's compact gloom
smooths himself
circling gloriously
in lonely joy
Sphere equal everywhere
entirely without limit
smooths himself
circling in lonely joy

two branches do not spring from his back
he has no feet no quick knees
no part of sex
he is Sphere
equal to himself
entirely without limit
no Strife or Quarrel in his body
when huge Neikos leapt up
inside Sphere Cosmeg
reaching out to rule

now that his time
had sailed around
he marked out his own path
replacing Sphere's fat circle
one after another
all the limbs of Sphere shook

Earth

Earth   the center of Sphere

she meets the other roots
Fire   Rain   bright Air

their equal
in age and birth

anchoring herself in Love's
tight harbors of accomplishment

sometimes   stronger in one thing
sometimes   weaker in another

from the roots blood and all forms
of flesh sprang

          BAUBO
        the wombs [of Earth]

in her smooth cunts
pleasant Earth received
two of the eight parts of NESTIS
               gleaming Water
two from HEPHAISTOS
     Fire

they were born bones
the skeleton Harmony joined

you will see
in the crusty back of shellfish
in the trumpet mollusk
tortoise with his stone skin
how Earth lives on top of flesh

hedgehog bristles point up
men sprouted from Earth
like heads of lettuce

gentle Fire has a short-lived share of Earth
Air brings clouds
Sea   sweat of the Earth

Sun and Moon

you hardly ever see the rapid arms of the Sun

untroubled he
sends his light flashing back
toward Olympos

gathering his Fire
he sails a circle in the sky

turning around Earth
smoothly spinning
his borrowed light
like a wheel track
at the edge of a field

sending out arms
like darts

sweet Moon
empty-eyed blind Night

gentle Moon looks with Love
on the luminous circle
of the Sun her king

Sun's arm punches
her smooth face

he hammers her

throwing his fists like darts
you hardly ever see

owl-eye Moon scatters
Sun on Earth
darkening as much land
as her face covers

ambushing light
Earth makes night

Sun's shining body is veiled
you cannot see the hairy tribes of Earth or Sea

Men and Women

Fire
when he split in two
fashioned in the night
angular men
wailing women

whole born sketches of men
sprang up from earth
like head lettuce
half Heat half Water

Fire
eager to mate himself in them
lifted them to light

though they did not show
the lovely body of their limbs
and were without voice
man's mark

wrapped in sheepskin cauls

since men are born
in Earth's warmer wombs
they are darker than women
hairier   and have a cock

the human body's birth
is split between
the mother's and the father's

when a man's clear sperm leaves him
enters his wife
when she is cold
a female is born

Love

the divided meadows of Aphrodite
give life

Love   Friendship   Harmony

a kiss
her eyes serious

a knot binds two
two eyes see one

just as the juice of a fig
bolts white milk and rivets it

Aphrodite joins with bolts of Love
as wheat bound by Water makes bread

Water marries wine
she does not Love oil

yellow crocus' rays
meet and mingle in linen threads

desire steals over me
softening mixing
in the organs of my body

all that is thick inside
full of holes outside
receives a surplus of Water
from the hands of Love

after Love Watered Earth with rain
breathless she gave the bodies of the living
to homeless Fire for hardening

everything was in her hands
when it grew the first time

the Love-light in your soft eyes
threaded mine
two eyes see one

when you're going out on the road at night
you take a lamp
Fire against the evening storms
when winds blow
you raise the windscreen
to keep out the cold
but the light leaps over the lamp's rim
piercing night far as he can go
with unworn lance

this is how Love guards her storied Fire
locked in the body's membranes
she kindles him in a girl's glancing eyes
spinning a net of svelte linen of flesh
to protect the flame from Water's depths
that surround her pupil

but the light leaps over the rims of your eyes
piercing night far as he can go
with unworn lance

from the four roots
from the mixing and exchanging Air Fire Earth Water
grew the shapes and colors of all living things
Love joined in Harmony

from them she made
indestructible eyes

*"everything feels
and has a share of thought"*

from the roots
Love joined in Harmony
everything was made

through them
each thinks suffers rejoices

Earth sees Earth
Water Water
Air Air
Fire Fire
Love Love
Hate Hate

so on so forth forever

sweet fucks sweet
bitter plunges in and out of bitter
sharp cuts sharp
salt couples salt

so on so forth forever

turned toward what is before them
men's thought grows

come listen to me
understanding increases thought

thoughts spin on tides of blood
that ebb and flow
for that is where what people call thought is

blood around the heart
men's thought

everything breathes in and out
through bloodless pipes of flesh
stretched throughout the body

delicate furrows pierce the mouth
the surface of the skin
there blood pools
and Air cuts for himself
easy passage in and out

gentle blood sings in the veins
while it retraces its path
leaping back into the body's crevices
and the straight flow of Air enters
but when blood returns
Air breathes out

there are exhalations
from everything that has been born

dog's nose tracks
the slices of themselves
animals leave behind
breath from their paws
lingers in fresh grass

shadows darken the river bottom
your hollow eyes
because they are alike
see the black in caves

every thing partakes of breath smell and sight
longing to return to themselves in others

time sails in a circle

"everything that is born
feels and has a share of thought"

Natural Demonstration

Air makes the evergreen
fruitful all year long

tall olive trees lay eggs

pomegranates ripen late
running over with juice

Water from bark
steeped in wood
is wine

salt hardens
pushed back on itself
by the gleaming blows of the Sun

there are drugs
that overcome sickness and age

I have shown you all this
so you can test it

so you will master the unwearying winds
that spring up waste fields harrying Earth

that when you wish
call them back

to bring for men
after black rain
bright weather

after summer drought
make rain to feed the trees
as it falls from the skies

and bring back from hell
the life of the dead

HYMN TO PHANES WITH PROEM
FROM THE *ORPHIC ARGONAUTICA*

Stanza 1 is from the *Orphic Argonautica,* a Greek text from
the second century A.D., using materials from c. 800 B.C.
Stanza 2 is from the *Hymn to Phanes,* a Greek Orphic text,
c. third century A.D., which is a revision of an earlier hymn of
the sixth or seventh century B.C. The remainder of this selection
is from the *Orphic Argonautica.* All texts: Hermann, *Orphica.*

Lyre god Apollo
I will sing for you
a new song
I will reveal your terrible arrows
to all men everywhere
but especially to those
my rites have kept pure

When Time and wailing Need
split the ancient egg
out stepped Love the firstborn
fire in his eyes
wearing both sexes
glorious Eros
father of immortal Night
Phanes, god of Brightness
whom Zeus swallowed and brought back
Zagreus
Osiris
Dionysos
offer myrrh
Bull Shouter
laden with gold
Seed of gods and men
Priapos
Erikapeios
horned

clandestine
unnamed
Sounding Rusher
All Shining Slayer of Night in the eyes of men
everywhere on the pure oars of his wings
my lord
quick-glancing Reflector
Sparkler
Blessed Clever Ubiquitous
Go rejoicing in the completed acts of his name
In the countless wombs of Earth
Time brought forth Air
and the grim goddess Death
and the Strainers the Tighteners
who stay beneath boundless earth forever
because of what they did

Then Healer
and Mountain Mother
who fashioned Huntress Moon Queen
from relentless Sky Father son of Time

Have you heard of the mangling of Zagreus?
of the gods who lived on Mount Ida?
of MotherEarth who wandered in the great gulf
in search of her child to give us law?

the meaning of dreams

the reading of the signs

the star roads

the cleansings needed

atonement

satisfaction

the mountains of gifts the dead require

what I learned
when singing and playing
I followed the shadowy paths of hell
in search of love

when in Egypt
I gave birth to the stag
as I neared holy Memphis
and the round cities of Apis
the eddying Nile surrounds
where I was taught my secrets

you have learned all things unerringly from my heart
I have done it by sixes and sevens

now the gadfly leaves me
stinging and burning
my body learns from the unremitting sky

you will learn from my voice
all the things I concealed
from stubborn men
how the heroes and half gods
passed over into Peiria
and the steep sheer head of the Wet Country
praying that I would be their messenger
that I would guide the stroking of their oars
I the precursor of their return
in White Boat against the inhospitable nations
of rich and reckless people
against the claiming of their gold

I sail on the ship of the world

FROM HESIOD, *THEOGONY*
(THE VISION)

A Greek text, c. 600 B.C., taken from Hurrian-Hittite and earlier Indo-European forerunners dating from before 2300 B.C. Text: Hesiod, *Theogony* (West, ed.).

children of Zeus
grant me song
of the gods who are forever
who were born out of Earth and star-lit Sky
dark Night and Salt Sea

speak tell me
how we were born the beginning
of the ground we walk on
rivers ponds lakes
sea without end swelling rushing
stars sending light
sky cupped overhead
gods born of them
the gods givers of good things
dividing wealth among themselves
honors titles a palace in the mountains
Olympos

Muses living in the houses of Olympos
who was first?

"Gap was first
then Earth the great chair with her immense teat

then Pit hard to see
deep in the wombs of Earth

              next Love
                      loveliest of gods
             who unstrings the body
                          tames the heart
                    breaks the mind
                            whether god or man
                    within his heart

         the children of Gap were Gloom and Night
              whom Love joined
         their children were bright Air and Day

                      Earth's firstborn was star-lit Sky
                      a lover to cover her
                              equal in every particular

              he made her his chair
                  the seat forever for the happy gods

    the children of Earth
              the long hills where nymphs roam
                    who sleep in thickets
         sterile sea 'without sweet union of love'
               because his salt will not make her fruitful
                        in his swelling rushing
         Earth sheltered Sky
                    their children were the Earth-born the Geagants
               tidal Ocean
         sons Koios and Krois and Hyperion and Iapetos
    daughters Theis fixer Rhea flow-er Themis setter
         Mnemosyné recaller Phoebé with a golden crown
                              Tethys lady of the deeps

         her youngest Kronos 'air large birds ride'
                      thinks in crooked ways
                    most feared of all her family
                for in his energy he hated his father

                    the children of Earth
                         Wheel Eyes hearts of force
                              Thunder Lightning Thunderflash
they gave Zeus thunder they made him the thunder bolt
                    like all the gods in everything
          except for the one eye turning in their forehead
                    wheeling in place between their two eyes

          the three sons of Earth and Sky
                         never named proud Kottos Briareos Gyes
                              from their shoulders
                                   hundred hands leap forth
                              upon each of their shoulders
                                   fifty heads wag
                              upon their muscled bodies
                                   out of their shoulders
                    not according to nature
          unapproachable ungraspable in their strength
                         hated and feared most of all
                              as soon as they were born

                         as soon as his children were born
                              Sky hid them away
                         he deprived them of light
          shoving them back deep into the wombs of Earth
                              he went away and laughed

                              Earth crowded groaned
                    she thought of something clever and ugly
                 she made gray adamant
                              made a sickle of it
made her children understand what she wanted done with it
                         sorrowing in her heart
                    she encouraged them
                              'pay him back for what he has done
                                   he was first to hurt'
                    this is what she said

FROM HESIOD, "THEOGONY" (THE VISION)   315

they were afraid
                none of them answered
but great Kronos who thinks around corners was not afraid
                he spoke to his wise mother
                'I shall do it
                I shall finish it
                I do not love my father
                he was first to hurt'
        he spoke huge Earth shook with joy in her heart
                she hid him in a place of ambush
        she put the sickle with jagged teeth in his hand
                she showed him her plan

                great Sky came
                        bringing night
                lying heavy on Earth in love and desire
        she opened receiving him
their son stretched out his left hand from ambush
in his right he held the great sickle with jagged teeth
                he chopped off his father's balls
                        he threw them to the wind behind him
                they flew away a bloody track in the air
                        which Earth enfolded
        in full time she gave birth to the strong Curses
                        and the great Titans
        full-armored bursting with light shaking long spears
                and the Meliads nymphs of the ash tree
                        all over boundless Earth

when his balls cut down by adamant
fell from boundless Earth
onto high Sea
battered they swam open currents
from that deathless flesh foam blossomed
inside the pink flower a girl was born and grew
she passed by holy Cythera
she came to Cyprus surrounded by water's flood
she stepped onto land
august lovely goddess
grass sprung up under her tapered feet
Aphrodite born of foam Cytheria the well-garlanded
because she grew inside the bloody foam
because she passed near Cythera
Cyprogene because there she was born
on Cyprus wave washed
Philomedes because she loves Love's bone
because she was born inside her father's balls
Love walks with her
Desire follows

as soon as she was born
she went right to the race of gods
this is the honor she holds this is what they allotted her
her share among men and deathless gods
young girls' talk
their laughter and sweet deceit
delight pleasure lovemaking softness

the sons great Sky fathered he cursed
calling them Titans the Strainers
because he said they tightened and strained
to do proud deeds
and they would be paid back for it soon afterward"

FROM APOLLODORUS, THE *LIBRARY*
(GENEALOGICAL CATALOG)

A genealogical catalog from the Greek text by Apollodorus, c. third century B.C.–first century A.D., taken from a pre-Hesiodic source in Greek, which was derived from earlier Indo-European sources. Text: Apollodorus, *Bibliotheca* (Frazer, ed.).

Ouranos was first king of the ordered world
he married Gea

their first children were the Hundred-handed
        Briareus
        Gyes
        Kottos
they were impossibly big and strong
they had a hundred hands a hundred heads

their next children were the Cyclops
        Arges
        Steropes
        Brontes
each had one eye in the middle of their forehead
Ouranos tied them up and threw them into Tartaros
a dark place in Hades as far from earth
as earth is from sky

their next children were the Titans
        Okeanos
        Koios
        Hyperion
        Kreios
        Iapetos
        Kronos youngest of all

their daughters were the Titanides
> Tethys
> Rhea
> Themis
> Mnemosyné
> Phoebé
> Dioné
> Theia

Gea wept because Ouranos destroyed their children
he tied them up and threw them all into Tartaros
Gea persuaded the Titans to fight their father
she gave Kronos a sickle of adamant
all the Titans except for Okeanos fought Ouranos
Kronos cut off his balls and threw them out to sea

from the drops of his blood the Erinyes were born
> Alecto
> Tisiphoné
> Megaira

the Titans took away their father's kingship
they freed their brothers from the dark place of Tartaros
they gave the kingship to Kronos

Kronos tied them all up and threw them again into Tartaros
he married his sister Rhea

Ouranos and Gea told him
a son of his would take away his kingship
he swallowed his children as soon as they were born

he swallowed his first child
> Hestia

he swallowed
> Demeter
> Hera
> Pluto
> Poseidon

Rhea was enraged
she went to Crete carrying Zeus
she gave birth to him in a cave of Dicté
she gave him to the Kouretes to protect
to the brides Adrasteia and Ida to nurse
the brides fed him milk of Amaltheia
the Kouretes guarded the cave
banging swords on their round shields
so Kronos would not hear the voice of his child
Rhea wrapped a stone in baby blankets
and gave it to Kronos to swallow
she said it was Zeus

when Zeus grew up
he took Metis daughter of Okeanos to help him
she gave Kronos a drug to swallow
it made him throw up the stone
then the children he had swallowed

Zeus fought Kronos
his brothers and sisters helped
Gea said Zeus would win
if all those Kronos threw into Tartaros helped
Zeus killed their jailer Kampé
he smashed their chains

the Cyclopes gave Zeus thunder lightning and the thunder bolt
they gave Pluto a helmet Poseidon a trident

the children of Kronos used their weapons
they beat the Titans
they defeated their father
they tied them up and threw them into Tartaros
they chose the Hundred-handed to guard them

they threw lots for the kingship
Zeus won the kingdom of the sky
Poseidon the kingdom of the sea
Pluto the kingdom of Hades

Zeus married Hera
their children were
                    Hebé
                    Eileithuia
                    Ares

Zeus fucked many goddesses and many girls

his daughters by Themis daughter of Ouranos were the Horai
                    Eirené
                    Eunomia
                    Diké

also the Moirai
                    Klotho
                    Lachesis
                    Atropos

his daughter by Dioné was Aphrodité

his daughters by Eurynomé daughter of Okeanos were the Graces
                    Aglaia
                    Euphrosyné
                    Thaleia

his daughter by Styx was Persephoné

his daughters by Mnemosyne were the Muses
                    Kalliope first
                    then Kleio
                    Melpomené
                    Euterpé
                    Erato
                    Terpsichoré
                    Ourania
                    Thaleia
                    Polymnia

THE SETHIAN CREATION STORY

The Sethian creation story according to Hippolytos, c. third century A.D. The Sethians were a Jewish Gnostic sect active in the first century B.C.–first century A.D. Text: Hippolytos, *Refutatio* (Wendland, ed.).

1. *the 3 of beginning: light, dark, spirit*

> spirit where light and dark void each other
> clear and unconfounded
> > no wind blowing gentle breeze
> ointment or perfume
> > it steals into things
> > > better than words

> light above dark below spirit between

> > light the sunray on dark beneath
> in molten fire everywhere incenses
> > the subtleties of spirit
> to lead powers of both alive
> into dark whose fearful water drinks light
> > in spirit essence
> thinks and thinks over
> > if light leaves
> she knows herself isolate
> > invisible shrouded asleep heartless inert
> > willing her to assemble within
> > > glints and chromes of light
> > > to the spirit's lifting

> (image:
> > the eye's vitreous dark
> > spirits light
> > > down its black hole)

                    patrolling for light
                          dark desires outward splendor to see
                                and bind his emissaries
                                      freckling night sea

          light and spirit
                    empower themselves to stand
                                toward each other
                                      embracing
                                plunging into dark
                                      the strong down water

2. *the seals*

              all powers of the 3 of beginning
                                number countlessly
                          thinking and thinking again
                                while alone they rest

        should a power close another
                    self lawed by difference to strike

                    this marks both
                          sealing stamped figures

        doing this over and over
                    forging endless seals
                    that type everything that lives

3. *womb*

              the first marking of the 3
                    coined womb
                          in character newly jammed open by cock
              she the great seal of heaven and earth
                          circling midway omphalos
                                the navel stone
                          (counterpart:
                                any womb a child quickens
                          swallows a size of heaven
                                and earth
                                      sitting changelessly
                                      on cunt stool)

when earth and sky close in womb
they seal the powers of the 3
striking them off beyond number
in body of wombs
shredding into type
tiles of light odors of spirit

4. *wind*

from dark
from water her oldest
boisterous wind
beginner who enforces all birth
in sea foam
turning out waves
dances in them
child shivering their wombs
impelling man or mind
to well up
in the source of their coming forth
taken as ocean is
when spirit kicks
showering headlong

every wave wind tears from water
and puts child into
buds within power of woman of birth
fleshing in the new life
splintered light
spirit stealth

5. *the god of this world*

the new life this sunray of wave
is a finished god
generation bears down
wind blows to birth his temple

                    woven in water
                        he lights dark
                            mixes and mingles in bodies
                                salting them
        fighting
            helpless to break the bonds of type
                        no exit no liberty
                            from the charnel house of womb
                        broken spark
                            slivered splinter star seed
                    compacted in the reused bodies of many
                    the voice of the lord is upon the waters
                    the god of glory thunders
                    the lord is upon many waters
        schemes worries
                        how to escape death
                            and kill the dark sod body
                        father wind who is below
                            roaring and swelling
                                stamped him with
                        knocking up waves
                        making the perfect mind of light
                            his not-of-his-body son

    god of this world
            wind child glancing from bright thought
                    eye of spirit borne down in water
            churning in dark the torn cunted fear-bitter sea

6. *manchild*

    once wind has desired the waves in spirals out of ocean
                blowing within them
                        power of women of generation
            their wombs swallow every kind and gender
                            where light sticks
                    so that whatever they strike
                        barbs dark and is seen

the fury wind of night whirling strength in his fear
                    turns the hissing dyne snake
          cyclone serpent daddy of birth
                    seals the whirled
               marking everything at once
          funneling light and spirit home
     into the cruel disordered womb of curse
                    fathering there manchild
               for the danced water womb
                    set of many waves
          does not love or open for any strike of flesh
                              but snake's

7. *word*

          to retell this story
                    the perfect word of light
               in serpent's body beast
                         cheats the womb
                    coming as her cherished
               disposed as her counterfeit the snake

     fathered in womb's cloaked trench
               by water's oldest the serpent/wind/beast
          word breaks the chains that bind the mind
     for *himself of no reputation he took upon himself*
     the form of a servant and was made in the body of men
          but not enough his journey down into a virgin's womb
                         laboring in that darkness
     he must drink opening the door the womb's secret pain
               and be washed *in the well of water*
                         springing up into everlasting life

This is a cosmology from the Ophites (Naasenes), a Jewish Gnostic sect of snake-worshipers active from the first century B.C. through the second century A.D. Text: Hippolytos, *Refutatio* (Wendland, ed.).

1. Naas The Serpent Whom We Wear

you can   make   **7**   from the brain

vaulted room

wings   on either side
wind blows on

through blood pipes

to Pine Nut

down   Spine Sperm

tailing in cock cunt

where brain kern sleeps in secret blood

this is in small Serpent Naas   who made us

brain the dragon head
six other coiling lines from there
bind the corpse
spine   containing the well-head   the stinging tail
the seventh

2. Naas The Great Man

"Who shall declare his generation?"

"Earth   mother   man   willing   a   good   gift
not   loving   the   wild   ones   only
but   devising   a
        thinking
        gentle
        and   lovely   one" :

        Alalcomenes in Boeotia near Lake Cephisis
        Koros of Ida of Crete   branch of the gods
        Korybas of Phrygia   whom the sun first saw
              jumping up like a tree from the mother
        Pelasgos from Arcadia   older than Moon
        Diaulos in Raria   mother: Eleusis the Free
        Kabiros of Lemnos   pretty Mystery child
        Alcyoneus from the Phlegaian Fields   oldest of the
              big Earth—born   mother: Pallené
        Iarbas   desert child   Libya   chewing Zeus nuts
        Nile   making without fathermother
              mud rendering the living corpse
                  buying meat from water
        Oan of Assyria
        Adam from Chaldea   whom Earth alone enwombed

Naas stared down into the statue pool of self so hard it moved
        said :

LIVE   !   SUFFER   !   DIE
           punishing   the slave image
              over—mastered by what heshe saw
     The Great Man names the whole family of Earth and Sky
            to where we struggle to escape

3. Soul

        What The Great Man did to the statue of many and single name
           is called

                  SOUL

        which makes all things and makes them grow

                              even stones
                     for they undergo increase
                     accession
                     the food that feeds us all
          Soul   a 3   and a 1
                                        the names of soul
                              according to the AsSyrians
                         :
                              Adonis
                              Endymion
                              (Attis)

soul Adonis
                     Venus loves
                                   and desires
                     for she is natural increase

soul Adonis
                     Koré or Persephone loves
                              then Adonis leaves Venus
                                   and parts from generation

soul Endymion
                     when Moon passes into love for him
                              desires to remove "above"
                                        is demanded and
                                        responds into life

when the mother of the gods cuts off the balls of Attis
                                        yet loves him anyway
it is because The Great Man has recalled the male from him
                     Adonis lives
                having surrendered the parts of earth
                              to the unconsummated world "above"
                              "where there is neither Jew nor Greek

                     bond or free

                     male or female :
                     for all are one in Jesus Christ"

                     a new man   a malefemale

4. "Above"

Lady Change   Mother of the Gods   is not alone
            Naas says and   Word agrees

                                              :

      "what you cannot see of The Great Man
                the world of creation does
          knowing   heshe is their author
                   their undying power"
      "for the purpose of leaving them without excuse"

the creatures that know do not thank him
                their hearts are emptied
        saying they are wise
                they become fools
  changing The Great Man in them to corpse man
    and birds and four-foot and crawling things

    so Great Man let them love one another
          each according to their self diminution
           the women stopped fucking
                the men left them

men playing with men   with the "unseemly" :
come   that first and happy substance
figureless   cause of all figures   that come into shape

      receiving in themselves the just payment for their mistakes

5. Logos Hermes

   :   Hermes   Cyllené's son   calls away the breath
      of those   who think back   on home
      in his hands   holds   a pretty golden   stick
            that soothes   the eye
                if he wants it   to
    but wakes   others   from death's sleep

with   the stick   makes passes   in the   air
their chirping breaths   churn   in answer   follow
into the   turns   of magic   cave like bats   children of   night
if one falls   from   shelving rock
the rest   stick together
like birds   the ghosts   in swirling flocks
chase   the wand
across Earth's   broad   roads   over Ocean's springs
and   White Rock Leuké
past   Sun Gate   and the   country   of dreams
perching in
fields of asphodel
where   souls wait
pictures   of those who   have done their   work and   died   :

Hermes the Cock
master of life and death
who awakens the sleeping to a recollection of self
conveying The Great Man from "above"
into   the   fiery creation of clay
to serve Ialdabaoth a 4
father of the formal world

Hermes the Christ
in all who have been generated
the figured Man Son
from figureless Logos

in Eleusis   "Hyé : Kyé"
Rain ZeusBacchus :   Get Big With Baby

when Ocean ebbs   then   :
a generation of men

but flooding   towards the Wall and Fortress
of White Rock Leuké
makes
a generation of gods

Ocean Jordan dividing Israel from Egypt

THE NAASENE COSMOLOGY   331

6. Naas The Great Man (II)

Matters if
you are   Titan   or   Zeus   or Lady Change   ?

Attis, dark tearing of the Mother of the gods
whom   :
AsSyrians call   —Adonis   longed-for 3 times
Egyptians   —Osiris   Moon's sky horn
Greeks   —   Sophia
Samothracians   —   Adam
Haemonians   —   Corybas
Phrygians   —   PAPA or Corpse or God   or
Fruitless or Green Wheat Kern
Reaped In Peace   or
Amygdalos' Child
a man a musician

I   want to sing to you, Attis, Lady Change's Son
not with roaring trumpets
skirling pipes of Ida of Crete
that fit so well
Kouretes' Chorus

I will join my song with Apollo's   harp
intoning

EVAN ! EVOE !

for you are Pan
:   Bacchus
herding the blinding stars

7. Naas The Serpent In The Garden

every one under heaven   : a temple/Naos of Serpent Naas
anywhere you do a holy thing
you enter   Naos   house of Naas

you cannot leave the temple of yourself
except to return to Naas

Naas　:　stream of Water　Ocean spring
　　　　　　　　horn of the one
　　　　　　　　one-horned bull
　　　　　　　　goring all in himherself
　　　　　　　　　　so that he gives them beauty and bloom
　　　　　　　　　　　　nature and peculiarity

Naas　:　River of Eden　dividing into four
　　　　　　　Eden the brain
　　　　　　　　　　　robed in seven : veils of
　　　　　　　　　　　　　　Isis of generation
　　　　　　　　　　　Paradise as far as the head

　　　　　　but coming in and out
　　　　　　　　　the four rivers

　　　　　:

Pishon　surrounding the land　Havilath
　　　　　　where there is gold
　　　　　　gold of that land excellent
　　　　　　bdellium and the onyx stone
　　　　　　　:
　　　　　　the eye
　　　　　　that by its colors
　　　　　　　　testifies to what is said

Gihon　river of Ethiopia
　　　　　　tortured labyrinth
　　　　　:
　　　　　the ear

Tigris　for Assyria
　　　　swift as breath　and smell of:nose
　　　　drawn and pushed forth in analogy

Euphrates　:
　　　　　　mouth for praise for food
　　　　　　　feeding and incorporating
　　　　　　　　The Great Man
　　　　　　　　　who is
　　　　　　"the water above the firmament"

" if you knew what to ask
　　　　he would give you living bubbling water "

into this water every breath enters choosing itself forming shape
                            peculiarity   desires   each nature
                                    more than iron   the magnet
                            or gold the sea falcon's backbone
                                    and chaff   amber

through Naas the blind man will see Paradise Park

                                            planted with every tree
                                            and fruit of the Tree

                    water sighing through the trees and fruits

will see from one and the same water

                                    olive tree drink
                                            and draw oil
                            vine curve down
                                            and find wine
                            so on and so forth forever

The Perfect Man is unknown in this world
                            betrayed by the ignorant
                            who are as a drop in a cask
                                    small dust in the balance pan

Pass through the third gate
                    receive the proof of things unseen
                            that who you are is all you are not

FROM OVID, *METAMORPHOSES*

From the *Metamorphoses* of Ovid, A.D. 9, from various earlier
sources. Text: Ovid, *Metamorphoses* (Proosdij, ed.).

before land was or sea or sky that covers all
    nature everywhere wore the same face
which you might call "chaos" raw unformed mass
    unharmonious ununion of the seeds of things
all crowded together into the same place
      all at war with each other
        all unaware
  the sun gave no light
    the moon did not lead out the months
earth did not spin in the void balanced by its weight
the ocean did not reach into the long shores of the land
    though there was land and sea and sky
you could not walk or swim or look into air that lacks light
      nothing knew form
    all stumbled into each other
  in one body they fought
cold with hot wet with dry soft with hard
  that without weight with that which did
      a god it was or must have been
    or a kindlier nature who stopped this war
  split land from sky sea from land
  the gassy heaven from thick heavy air
      freed them from blind chaos
bound them in their separateness by the concords of peace
      each in its own place
the force of fire weightless form of arched heaven leapt up
made a place for itself in the sky's highest tower
next to fire air lay second in lightness and station
next earth thicker than fire and air
    preserving the heavy elements
      pressed down by its own weight
last of all water embracing solid earth flows around it

when he whichever god it was
had so arranged chaos
reduced it divided it in sections into proper members
he englobed earth a perfect sphere
so it would be equal in every part
then ordered the sea to flow around it
and swell into waves at the wind's blast
breaking on the shores of the encircled continents
to them he added springs swamps lakes
ringed the rivers flowing down their steep banks
and set them far apart from each other
partly absorbed by earth
the rest rushing into the sea
emptying into the plains of a freer water
where they stroke beach instead of riverbank
now he ordered the fields to widen out valleys to sink
the forests to cover in leaf in stone the mountains to rise up
two zones divided the sky on the left
two on the right
so the universe set and grew hard in its place
god thought caused it to divide into two
the same number as before
and the same number of districts to be stamped on the earth
the one in the middle is too hot
snow covers the two at the poles
two others he put between the middle and the ends
and gave them temperateness heat mixed with cold
overhead lies the air
heavier than the zone of fire
in the same proportion as water is than land
there he ordered mist and cloud to take their places
and thunder shaking men's minds
and the winds that flash out in thunder bolts
the workman did not give them all the sky for their home
but even now it is difficult to prevent them
from lashing out against the world
although they each blow in a different part
such is their fraternal discord

the East Wind went off to the kingdom of dawn
to Nabataea and the mountains of Persia
made bright by the rays of Matin
the West Wind combs the land evening where the sun sets
the bristling North Wind sweeps through Scythia and the Northland
the country directly opposite
is made continually wet by the clouds of the rainy South Wind
over them he laid hazy air lacking weight
showing no trace of earthen dung
he had hardly separated things into their fixed orbits
when the stars blocked by blind mist
grew to shining through the sky
so that no place in the universe would be without its own form of life
stars and god shapes peopled the heavenly earth
water made a home for silvery fish
land sheltered the animals
air fit for flying the birds
a living thing holier than all these capable of higher mind
to be master of all was as yet lacking
Man
whether the workman created him from divine seed
a race from a better world
whether the fresh earth just separated from the lofty fire
preserved some fragments of heaven
which Prometheus mixed with rain water
molding it in the likeness of the gods who rule over everything
is unknown
in any case Man came into existence
while all other living things down cast stare at the ground
he gave man a high face
told him to look up at the sky to lift his head to the stars
this is how the universe which only moments before
had been unformed without image
changing aspect took upon itself form and forms strange till then

FROM OVID, *FASTI*

From the *Fasti* of Ovid, A.D. 16, taken from native Italian sources. Text: Ovid, *Fasti* (Frazer, ed.).

January First the Calends

               dawn
          the senate and people unlock his temple

                  sky burns with new fire
             saffron sparkles on the fire place
    flame beats on the temple's gold—new-won splendor

                kind words now
       no arguing—look what it did before

in untarnished white the procession moves towards the hill
               wearing the color of the day

           new rods of office
         new purple on their cloaks
who's that sitting on the ivory chair—never saw him before

             priests stretch the cow's neck

                 ax falls

     Janus alone looks back

        flooding the room with light
             two heads two faces
      staff in his right hand
       key in his left

the mouth facing front speaks

"long ago they called me Chaos
                    that's how old I am

fire air earth water were one

                    argument split them

fire went up

        air in the middle

earth and water sank down

                all found new homes

        then I
    up 'til then Sphere
            shape without image
    took on face and body of a god

now just to remind you I was Chaos
        I look the same back and front

            there's another reason—listen

    whatever you see—sky sea clouds land
                    I open and close with my hand
            I guard/regard the world
        law of the wheeling hinge is mine
    I unlock war and peace
                I sit in front of the gates of heaven
        with the kindly Hours
                    Day-Father comes and goes
                            I meter him

priests feed me cookies of barley and spelt
                    mixed with salt
                         call me funny names Opener Closer
               but that's the way it is
         every door has two sides
                         one facing the people
               the other the Lar inside

     porter of heaven's door I see East and West
                         who goes in and out

                              Hecaté has three faces
               so she can watch three roads meet
     me too—so I won't waste time
         I look two ways without turning"

          "why does the year begin in winter?

                    why not in spring

          flowers

          time made new

                    vines puffed out
          tree fingering her green hems
                         wheat bearding earth
                    birds twittering winnowing air
               cattle living it up out in the fields
                              then sunlight is sweet
                    swallow returns
                    builds her nest of clay
                              under the roof beam

                    plow sow do it all again
               why not then?"

"in two words: winter sunstill—one sun ends another begins
     Phoebus and the new year start up together"

FROM VERGIL, ECLOGUE #6

From Eclogue #6 by Vergil, c. late first century B.C., is taken from Hellenistic and Roman sources, c. 400 B.C. or later. Text: Vergil, *Omnia Opera* (Papillon and Haigh, eds.).

Forward, Muses

the boys Chromis and Mnasyllus slunk into Silenus' cave
where they found him sleeping off a drunk
veins overblown by wine
garlands in petal flakes all around him
his well-worn drinking cup snoozing in one hand
               dangling by the handle

he'd promised them the song of the making of the world
but hadn't made good his word

so they chained him up
Aeglé helped
        (ah Aeglé, prettiest of them all)
she painted the top of his head
with blood red mulberries while he watched

"let me go, fellas,
you'll get your song
and later on
she'll get hers"

    then he sang
and then you would have seen Fauns and every wild thing
dance to the numbers in his voice
the stiff oak swaying her top

"the seeds that flower earth, wind and sea
        water as well as fire
               drove through the great void
from these primes
     everything began
   the soft circle of world

                    grew together
              farmland hardened
                    locking at sea the Sea Father
           the pretty shapes of things taking form
                              bit by bit
           rain falling clouds jammed together overhead
                    now the first time   woods spring
                         here and there
                              beasts roamed the unknowing hills"

and then he sang about us
     born from the stones Pyrrha   threw over her shoulder
          Italians living in Italy Saturn's golden land

and then about the vulture in the Caucasus
               who bites Prometheus in his passion
                    because he stole god fire

Appendix

Numerical Creation Texts

(SCHOOL OF) PYTHAGORAS,
THE WORLD OF NUMBERS

These Greek stories dating from the seventh–sixth century B.C. were part of the teachings of the school of Pythagoras and were collected by various ancient writers. The fragments used are numbered as follows: 1. Galen, *Historia Philosophica,* in Diels, *Doxographi Graeci;* 2. Aetius, *Placita* II 63–65, in Diels; 3. Philolaus, fragment 12, in Diels-Kranz, *Die Fragmente der Vorsokratiker;* 4. Parmenides, fragment 37, in Diels-Kranz; 5. Aristotle, *De caelo* II.13; 293a 19; 6. Aetius, in Diels-Kranz, Vol. I, 454 41ff.; 7. Aristotle, *Metaphysics* I.5; 8. Aetius, *Placita* I 3 8, in Diels; 9. Aristotle, *Physics* IV.6; 10. Aristotle, *Metaphysics* XII.6; 11. Aetius, *Placita* I 7 18, in Diels; 12. Aristotle, *Metaphysics,* 1.5; 13. Hippolytus, *Philosophumenon* 2.3–.18, in Diels; 14. Hermias, *Irrisio Gentilium Philosophorum* 16, in Diels; 15. Aristotle, *Nichomachean Ethics* II.5.

1.   —3 D—

the numbers
as Pythagoras proposed them

out of the cube
earth
out of the pyramid
fire
out of the octahedron (* * *)
water
out of the dodecahedron
the Sphere of all

2.   *or*

out of the octahedron
air
out of the icosahedron
water
out of the dodecahedron
Sphere

3.   there are five of Sphere
                      earth fire water air inside
                 Sphere the barge makes five

4.   at the center (of Sphere)
                   Fire

5.   Guard of Zeus
                   the daimon of direction
                      who holds the keys
                 Right and Need

4.   Earth star
               circles Guard

       for Night and Day

6.   now the nature of number is ten
   everybody counts to ten
               and then goes back to   one

7.   so there are ten stars
                   but you only see nine
       the tenth the counter-earth you cannot see
             (it is always behind Guard?)

8.   number makes

9.   empty cuts

10.   #1
       the only one

11.   #1 the god
                       who is the birth of 1

                  #2 the uncertain the aorist
                       the evil

12.   the 2's which are ten

1	2
end	endless
odd	even
one	many
right	left
male	female
stop	go
straight	bent
light	dark
good	bad
square	elongated

          pairs begin

13.   number is first
           the aorist the unholdable
                    that holds all numbers in endless
             numbers down to many

Pythagoras was four
before he was five

1. Aithalides pilot of the *Argo*
2. Euphorbos who fought at Troy
3. Mermotimos the Samian
4. Pyrrhos the Delian
5. Pythagoras

so   you do not die
you leap from one to another

what did Pythagoras   learn from Zaratas the Chaldean?

"daddie and mommie did it

he is light
she is shadow

warm	dry	light	fast	daddie
cold	wet	heavy	slow	mommie

the world is sexed in two's

harmony

sun's circle is music

two gods

sky demon	who is fire	sharing air warm and cold
earth demon	who is water	(sharing sweet and salt?)

one makes heaven grow
the other earth

#1	fathernumber	
#2	woman	even
#3	male	odd
#4	female	even

all numbers are fours

which makes ten the completed number

$$1 \quad + \quad 2 \quad + \quad 3 \quad + \quad 4 \quad = \quad 10$$

holy tetraktys

'spring of the roots
of timeless birth'

. . .

the fours of ten
completed number
are
1. number
2. monad
3. power
4. cube

interlacing 'mixing and mingling'

power	×	power	=	powerpower
power	×	cube	=	powercube
cube	×	cube	=	cubecube

and so on

until there are all numbers
fathermothering everything

                    but only seven shapes
number   monad   power   cubepowerpowerpowercubecubecube
           don't worry   —can't hurt you or get you dirty

                    they are you
                    and everything else

        don't forget
                    don't eat beans

                                why?
                            —listen

                    when the world was born
                        so was the bean

                    how can you   tell?

        if you chew a bean until it's pulp
                then put it under the sun for a while
                        it'll smell like come

            a better way of finding out—

                        take a bean when it's blooming
                        put it and its flower in a jug
                            bury for a few days

            know what you'll find?

                                a womb in the jar
                    a baby's head inside"

• • •

            Pythagoras also said

                    "stay quiet"

            he made them stay in little rooms
                            underground

14.

15.   I give   you give   that is justice

A Greek text, c. third century A.D., drawn from Egyptian
sources, c. third–fourth century B.C. Text: Hippolytos,
Refutatio (Wendland, ed.).

$$
\begin{array}{c}
\text{one} \\
\#1 \\
+1: \\
2 \\
+1: \\
3 \\
+1: \\
4 \\
\hline
10
\end{array}
$$

10—beginning number: ending it as well—   1

		10	=	1	
10	×	10	=	100	=	1
100	×	10	=	1000	=	1
1000	×	10	=	10000	=	1

the atomic
numbers: 3 5 7 (9(

7 = the orbit of 6 days plus 1

2
4
8 kindred

according to position
and division

```
1  =  Fire
2  =  Air
3  =  Water
4  =  Earth
```

god made the   world   a malefemale

fire and air   halfsphere of 1

blissful   rising   male

water and earth   halfsphere of 2

girlish   wanton   willful

fire and air   in 1

male and female

make the diacosm grow

```
fire  :  male
air   :  female
```

but look at this :

```
water  :  male
earth  :  female
```

therefore :

```
fire      powers      air
water                 earth
```

. . .

subtract   9
        from any number—they will end properly
                        some in 1—male
                        some in 2—female

$$\bigcirc \quad = \quad 360'$$
$$= \quad 40 \times 9$$

1   2
Fire   Air

$$= \quad 4 \ \times 90$$

3   4 $= \quad 360'$
Water   Earth

$$= \quad \bigcirc$$

light $= \quad 1$

dark $= \quad 2$

" and life to light, according to nature, and death to the duad
and to life, justice; and to death, injustice "

therefore : whatever the male numbers
produce is good

but the children of
female numbers
are mischievous

example :

361 — 9's = 1

605 — 9's = 2

you can compel   each number to reveal its reverted function

Selected Bibliography

Texts (many with commentary and translation into some modern language)

1. J. Burnet, *Early Greek Philosophy.*
2. R. H. Charles, *The Apocrypha and Pseudepigrapha of the Old Testament.*
3. G. Friedlander, *Pirke de Rabbi Eliezer.*
4. Th. Gaster, *Thespis.*
5. H. L. Ginsberg, *The Legends of Canaan.*
6. H. G. Güterbock, *The Song of Ulikummi.*
7. R. Haardt and J. F. Hendry, *Gnosis, Character and Testimony.*
8. A. Heidel, *Babylonian Genesis.*
9. Hesiod, *Theogony,* N. O. Brown (ed.).
10. J. Pritchard, *Ancient Near Eastern Texts.*
11. N. Sandars, *Poems of Heaven and Hell from Ancient Mesopotamia.*
12. E. A. Speiser, *Genesis* (in the Anchor Bible).

Secondary works

1. W. F. Albright, *Yahweh and the Gods of Canaan.*
2. M. Astour, *Hellenosemitica.*
3. V. Bérard, *Did Homer Live?*
4. The Cambridge Ancient History, Third edition, Vols. 1–4.
5. E. Dhorme and R. Dussaud, *Les anciennes religions orientales* (11).
6. C. Doria, "Introduction to the Phoenician History" (in *Io,* #6).

7. ——, "The Dolphin Rider" (in Macintyre [ed.], *Mind in the Waters*).
8. ——, "Commentary to Justin's *Baruch*" (in *Panjandrum,* #8).
9. ——, "Commentary on *Enoch*" (in *Io,* #21).
10. M. Eliade, *The One and the Two.*
11. A. Erhardt, *In the Beginning.*
12. H. Frankfort, *The Intellectual Adventure of Ancient Man.*
13. ——, *Ancient Egyptian Religion.*
14. K. Freeman, *The Pre-Socratic Philosophers.*
15. C. Gordon, *Homer and the Bible.*
16. W. C. Guthrie, *Orpheus and Greek Religion.*
17. E. Havelock, *Preface to Plato.*
18. P. Houwink Ten Cate, *The Luwian Population Groups of Lycia and Silicia Aspera During the Hellenistic Period.*
19. E. O. James, *The Tree of Life.*
20. ——, *Creation and Cosmology.*
21. S. N. Kramer, *Mythologies of the Ancient World.*
22. S. Moscati, *The Face of the Ancient Orient.*
23. C. Olson, "A Century or So Before 2000" (in *Maximus IV, V,* and *VI*).
24. R. Patai, *The Hebrew Goddess.*
25. —— and R. Graves, *Hebrew Myths.*
26. M. Ramnoux, *La nuit et les enfants de la nuit.*
27. G. Scholem, *Jewish Gnosticism, Merkabah Mysticism and Talmudic Tradition.*
28. M. L. West, *Early Greek Philosophy and the Orient.*